THE ACQUISITION MATING DANCE

and Other Essays on Negotiating

THE ACQUISITION MATING DANCE

and Other Essays on Negotiating

James C. Freund

Illustrations by Joseph Azar

PRENTICE HALL LAW & BUSINESS

Requests for permission to make copies of any part of the
work should be mailed to:

Permissions, Prentice Hall Law & Business
855 Valley Road, Clifton, NJ 07013

Printed in the United States of America

Library of Congress Cataloging-in-Publication Data

Freund, James C., 1934—
    The acquisition mating dance and
other essays on negotiating.
    Includes index.
    1. Consolidation and merger of corporations—
United States.   I. Title.
KF1477.F69 1987   346.73'06626   87-7342
ISBN 0-13-003807-5 347.3066626

    PRENTICE HALL LAW & BUSINESS
855 VALLEY ROAD, CLIFTON, N.J. 07013

To my wife,
    Barbara Fox Freund,
    Negotiator <u>par</u> <u>excellence.</u>

If my professional reputation
    were measured by the outcome
    of our bargaining sessions,
    I doubt that I'd
    have a single client. . . .

PERMISSIONS

Permission to reprint the following articles, in an adapted form, is gratefully acknowledged:

Planning A Negotiation? Start With Your Client, *Legal Times*, 11/5/84.

A Turbulent Decade for Friendly Deals, *National Law Journal*, 11/11/85.

Friendly Deal Requires Acquisition Mating Dance, *Legal Times*, 10/14/85.

Wearing Many Hats, *National Law Journal*, June 30,1986.

The Crucial Question: Who Wants the Deal More?, *Legal Times*, 8/5/85.

Lying in Negotiations Can Be Perilous, *Legal Times*, 6/3/85.

Back to Basics: Is There a Lawyer in the House?, *Legal Times*, 12/3/84.

Deadlocked Dealmakers Invoke Vegas Resolution, *Legal Times*, 2/6/84.

Getting to "Yes": Exploring Principled Negotiations, *Legal Times*, 3/10/86.

Comrade, Let's Talk This Over for Just a Minute, *Legal Times*, 3/4/86.

When the Playing Field Tilts: Negotiating Leverage in Acquisitions, *Insights*, 7/87.

The article "Bridging Troubled Waters" is adapted from an article which originally appeared in 12 *Litigation* No. 2 at 43 (Winter 1986); published by the Section of Litigation, American Bar Association.

CONTENTS

INTRODUCTION

Sam Goldwyn, the legendary Hollywood producer — the same Sam Goldwyn who uttered the immortal line, "A verbal contract isn't worth the paper it's written on" — was negotiating a deal one day with a certain actor.

"I'm asking fifteen hundred a week," declared the actor.

"You're not asking fifteen hundred a week," snapped Goldwyn; "You're asking twelve, and I'm giving you a thousand."

Well, that's one style of negotiating — pretty effective, I would imagine, under the virtual czardoms existing in Hollywood at the time. But that's the beauty of negotiating — there's room for a great variety of styles. For instance, dry sarcasm can be equally effective. Rudolph Bing, the former general manager of the Metropolitan Opera, disliked negotiations with the trade unions because of the hysteria and confrontations they generated. At one session with representatives of the stagehands, he leaned across the table toward the union lawyer and said,

"I'm actually sorry, I didn't get that. Would you mind screaming it again?"[1]

This book is a collection of essays about negotiating — about style and substance, some observations and a lot of quandaries, the real world and even a bit of fantasyland.

---

[1] The Goldwyn and Bing stories are borrowed from Fadiman, C., Ed., *The Little, Brown Book of Anecdotes* (Boston, 1985).

Negotiating is what I do for a living; and the notions that blossomed into these pieces arose in the context of representing a client in actual bargaining, or strategizing, or teaching a course to lawyers or law students, or just daydreaming about the subject.

I enjoy negotiating for clients — enjoy it more than any other lawyering activity I perform. In reflecting on why that's so, the analogy I keep coming back to is tennis vs. golf.

I prefer playing tennis to golf for a number of reasons — not least being that you don't have to suffer quite so long with your mistakes! — but the reason that's pertinent here is the presence in a tennis match of an interactive opponent. Sure, you face one or more adversaries in golf, but they don't really have much impact on the execution of your shots — the real culprits are the course, the clubhead and that little white ball. But in tennis, every move you make (except for your serve) is based on what your adversary has done, is doing and can be expected to do. If, for example, he hits a forcing shot deep to your backhand and starts in toward the net, and you anticipate (from prior experience) that he's likely to crowd you down the line, then you can eliminate most of the logical possibilities for your return shot — you'll either have to pass him cross-court or go over his head with a lob.

Well, it's the same quality that makes negotiating so interesting. So much of what you do in this arena is based on a necessarily imperfect subjective judgment — extrapolating from your adversary's past actions as to what his future conduct is likely to be — what's likely to appeal to him, or rile him, what you can sneak by his guard, and when is the best time to do it? Conversely, a lot of your time is spent worrying about what your adversary is trying to put over on you — what hidden clinkers exist in his apparently reasonable demands, what time bomb lurks in his seemingly neutral contractual language. And it's not just the *lawyer* on the other side whom you have to read, but his client, too (a task made more difficult by the other lawyer's skill at protecting him from you!).

All this makes for a fascinating exercise — and particularly when coupled with a stimulating subject matter (such as exists in my particular field of mergers and acquisitions). And it calls into play a number of skills not taught in law school or typically experienced in other areas of practice. You need to be alert to individual motivations, to strategic planning, to the concept of bartering, and so on.

For reasons I'll never understand, these are skills that many lawyers refuse to take seriously. But they should — it's part of what the client's paying for. If you could have produced a better deal for your client through more effective bargaining, but didn't, then your performance leaves something to be desired — no less so than if you had drafted papers which unwittingly created legal problems for the client.

Speaking of clients, that's another absorbing aspect of negotiating. The interaction with your own client — your ability to convey to him the sense of where the deal is heading, to grasp his vital interests, and to help him steer a reasonable course — is basic to your success. Moreover, these contacts take place on a level that's generally more satisfying (but can be more irritating) than in other areas of practice.

Let's face it, there are some areas in which the lawyer performs almost like a physician — in effect, *telling* the client what he *must* do if the client wants to accomplish his ends while staying on the right side of the law. The client has to take the lawyer's word for it — expertise carries the day. But briefings on negotiations usually take place on a much more basic level. Since the issues are understandable by laymen, and the client makes the ultimate decisions, he has to be actively involved in formulating and approving all matters of strategy. This can really put a lawyer on his mettle — particularly with a client who simultaneously makes unreasonable demands while charging the lawyer with ensuring that the deal happens. You know the refrain: "Get it cheap, but get it!"

Finally, there is something very satisfying about playing a role in a consummated deal. Most of the time, neither party *had* to agree, so it's really an expression of their free will — and since they started off disagreeing about so many matters, and there seemed dozens of obstacles to overcome before arriving at that final handshake, it's terrific to feel that you helped cause the deal to occur.

Of late, more and more of my professional writing and teaching has been in this largely neglected area. And although I've written on this topic elsewhere in somewhat more depth,[2] these twelve essays — while not purporting to be comprehensive — do touch upon certain key themes that I find myself returning to repeatedly in practice and teaching.

First is the importance for lawyers of being able to deal effectively with *their own client.* I find that most deals get made only if the client is persuaded of the need to take reasonable positions and propose meaningful concessions — inspiring reciprocal moves from the other side. This calls for real communication between lawyer and client. The piece, *Negotiating with Your Own Client,* explores the problem of a client who won't level with his lawyer as to what his top price (or bottom line) really is. It's a little game that businessmen like to play with their advisors,

---

[2] Freund, J., *Anatomy of a Merger — Strategies and Techniques for Negotiating Corporate Acquisitions* (Law Journal Press, 1975), particularly Chapter 2; and Freund, J., *Lawyering — A Realistic Approach to Legal Practice* (Law Journal Seminars-Press, Inc., 1979), particularly Section 7.3.

which can produce bad results in the negotiations. I offer some advice on how to handle this touchy issue.

As a lawyer, my particular area of concentration is mergers and acquisitions — enormously fertile ground for the would-be negotiator. The next four essays deal with some special aspects of M&A practice.

- The world of the mid-80's — spurred by the enormous destabilizing influence of hostile takeovers and other forms of financial coercion — is quite different from what existed in the mid-70's and earlier. The rules of the acquisition game for public companies have changed — not least in the different ways friendly deals get done and the agenda for (and styles of) meaningful negotiations. *A Turbulent Decade for Friendly Deals* charts these sea changes — the current emphasis on "done deals," multi-step trans-actions, tender offers, hybrid consideration, lock-ups, speed; the worry about what's "out there" rather than the insularity of what's "in here" — while cautioning practitioners not to forget that, amid this welter of technique, an acquisition is still a deal between two parties with plenty of room for creative negotiating.

- One significant byproduct of the times is the increas-ing number of acquisition situations — often involv-ing hostile takeovers — where a real disparity in bargaining leverage exists between the two sides. Many of the negotiating principles and tactics appli-cable to a level playing field aren't well-suited to these unbalanced circumstances. *When the Playing Field Tilts: Negotiating Leverage in Acquisitions* explores the main factors which create this imbalance — necessity, desire, competition and time — and counsels lawyers on how to assess the situation, deal with apparent leverage, cope with weakness and bargain from strength.

- The complexities aren't limited to hostile takeovers. For example, initiating friendly negotiations, while relatively straightforward in many instances, can sometimes be very tricky. *The Acquisition Mating Dance* traces the intricate choreography that often accompanies an attempt by a potential acquiror (who is unwilling to initiate a hostile takeover but not averse to exerting some pressure) to get a dialogue going with a publicly-held target company (which is bent on remaining independent but recognizes its fiduciary duty to the stockholders). This essay explores the tactical maneuvering — the approaches, the responses, the countermeasures, the various considerations — which the parties employ in today's corporate courtship.

- Lawyers who negotiate acquisitions have to play a variety of roles which go beyond traditional attorney functions, and for which they're rarely well-trained. *The Many-Faceted M&A Lawyer* focuses on the lawyer as financial whiz, psychologist, public relations consultant, generalissimo, seer, as well as some other roles that they never taught us about in law school.

Most bargaining situations in which lawyers play a role involve a unique item (a business, a property) being sold by a seller who doesn't *have to* sell (and without a specific price tag attached) to a buyer who need not buy (and who has access to alternative properties). One of the real keys to how the bargaining comes out furnishes the subject matter of the next piece: *Who Wants the Deal More?* Is it your client or the guy on the other side? And how strongly does each of them feel about it? This is the kind of motivational question, where the answer isn't always readily apparent (since a lot of posturing and self-deception goes on), that many lawyers fail to address — but they should, because a sense of the answer can help to shape the negotiations.

Most of my negotiating time is spent trying to put deals together — where the alternative to a successful conclusion is that one side or the other simply walks away and the process thereupon terminates. Lately, however, I've gotten involved in trying to resolve commercial disputes, both before and after litigation has begun. It's a whole new ball game, where the operative alternative to satisfactory resolution is trying the case — letting the judge or jury decide. *Bridging Troubled Waters* is a corporate lawyer's eye-opening initiation to the sticky problems — distrust, ambivalence, inscrutable prospects, to name a few — involved in trying to bring together warring factions, along with some practical advice that might prove helpful.

There's a school of thought that says tough positional bargaining is counter-productive — that the key to reaching agreement is to join with your adversary in a mutual problem-solving search for a wise outcome based on objective criteria. *The Outer Limits of Principled Bargaining* focuses on this approach in a familiar type of vendor dispute — a case in which I learned from my law school students that, depending on which side of the dispute he finds himself on, there may be limits to a negotiator's tolerance.

Information is crucial to a negotiator — in assessing what price will swing a deal, which arguments will persuade, what promises or threats are meaningful. Yet negotiators face a classic paradox: on the one hand, we strive for honesty and fairness in our dealings; on the other, we understand that not revealing of our true position or settling point may be critical to a successful outcome. Sometimes, these principles come into direct conflict, such that telling the truth will be clearly inimical to our client's interest. *Lying in Negotiations* explores the legal and ethical context in which we negotiate, and tries to grapple with difficult distinctions between permissible puffery and actionable misrepresentation.

Most of what we do as lawyers takes place in the comfortable confines of our offices — with full support systems operating and enough time to reach measured determinations. There are moments, though, when a lawyer is called upon to function on a more primitive level — when the business realities of the situation overwhelm the legal niceties. In business negotiations, this occurs when the two sides finally agree on the principal terms of their deal, and the client is determined to translate that handshake into a binding contract before the parties leave the table. *On Your Own in the Wee Hours* treats just such a deal, passing along a dozen tips that might prove useful if you wind up in a similar tight spot.

There's often a moment in bargaining where the parties are very close in price, but the protracted give-and-take has caused each party's position to rigidify — with the result that neither side is prepared to walk that final mile. Splitting the difference may seem the best solution but, for reasons explored in *The Vegas Resolution,* that's sometimes hard to accomplish without risk. This essay suggests a radical way to solve the problem — by rolling dice! Along the way, however, the craps approach manages to illuminate many of the concerns that arise in the final throes of making a deal.

Finally, I tried to envision the worst spot a negotiator could find himself in — where all the leverage seems to be pointing in the other direction and achieving even limited objectives takes every ounce of his bargaining wiles. *Negotiating with Nikita* is a fanciful treatment of just such a predicament — a prisoner with secret information, trying to bargain his way out of the clutches of the KGB, using techniques derived from situations involving less dire straits.

I hope these essays will both entertain and prove useful in your future negotiations.

J. C. F.

August 1987

NEGOTIATING WITH YOUR OWN CLIENT

LAWYER: *All right, George, you've told me that your goal is to buy the Jones property for $10 million. Now, before we decide what price to offer tomorrow in the initial negotiations, I'd like to know how much beyond that you're willing to go, just in case the other side isn't willing to sell at $10 million.*

CLIENT: *Oh, not very far at all. In fact, the $10 million is just about my upper limit.*

LAWYER: *Let me make sure I understand. The price you'd like to pay and your outside limit are the same number?*

CLIENT: *That's right.*

Here's a snippet of dialogue reminiscent of "the check is in the mail" to lawyers who regularly negotiate for their clients — doing deals, settling lawsuits, or whatever. It's the old story of a client who won't level with his lawyer as to what his top price (or bottom line) really is.

THE CLIENT'S LITTLE GAME

As a problem for the lawyer, this is not nearly as serious as the client who deliberately lies to his lawyer

11

about factual matters — who says, "There's no file," when the incriminating evidence exists. That bozo should be promptly thrown out of your office. A client who negotiates with his lawyer, by contrast, isn't venal; he's just indulging in a little game that businessmen like to play with their advisors and representatives. Unfortunately, however, the game can produce bad results in the negotiations — results that would be avoidable if the client were more candid.

This is one aspect of a broader negotiating topic: dealing with your own client. As a negotiator, I find this often takes more of my time than bargaining with the other side. The key to making deals lies in persuading clients to take reasonable positions and propose meaningful concessions — not to give away the store, but to inspire reciprocal moves on the other side. This is tough duty, at best, and even harder when the client doesn't take the lawyer into his confidence.

Why does it happen? I think it's because the client fears that once you know his top number (or bottom line), you'll zoom right to the limit in your zeal to make the deal. Perhaps he's had a bad experience, or has been exposed to popular folklore. Maybe he's equating lawyers with investment bankers, brokers, and others who have a direct monetary interest in seeing the deal get done. Or perhaps he's been influenced by the way some lawyers turn the upper limit of their fee estimate ("My fee will be in the $30,000 to $50,000 range") into a self-fulfilling prophecy.

So, the client likes to keep something in reserve — a little extra gas in his tank, so to speak. He figures that what you don't know won't hurt you, and you'll bargain harder to make the deal at a good price.

WHAT'S THE HARM?

That doesn't sound so unreasonable (which is why they do it). But I believe that to negotiate effectively for a client, you need to know his ultimate tolerance for pain. It helps you decide at what level to initiate the bargaining, what subsequent moves to make, and what characterizations to place on the initial price, the adversary's reaction, and your later proposals.

It also has a lot to do with the predictive function of lawyers. Let me offer an analogy. A few years ago, I had dinner one evening with a lawyer who practices in the white collar criminal area. He was indignant over the fact that the court had just changed the rules of the game on him. Previously, the sentence imposed for a guilty plea to a single offense in a multicount indictment had been cut and dried; now, it wasn't clear at all. My friend complained bitterly that this subverted one of the primary aspects of his lawyering role — what he called the "predictive function." He felt deprived of the ability to advise his client what he could expect as a result of his plea.

The same thing happens here. Once I've become involved in a negotiation, if my client wants to know how I think things will turn out, I'm usually willing to venture a prediction. That can be helpful to a client in assessing his options. If I don't know how much the client is willing to spend (or accept), I can't make that forecast with any confidence.

THE DOWNSIDE RISK

The premise implicit in all this is that there's some downside risk for the client if you stick at his ostensible limit, not knowing that you could actually bid higher (or take less). What's the downside? It's the concern that the other side will walk away from the deal — that a seller will sell to someone else (or just decide not to sell at all), or that a buyer will find another property. This is my basic operating assumption in most negotiations.

Now, if you find yourself in the enviable situation in which the other side has no options — he must do the deal and there's no one else to do it with — well, then there's much more reason for the buyer to stick to a price that's less than what he's willing to spend. In a situation like this, the client's lack of candor with his lawyer carries far less potential for harm. But, in most deals of consequence, the other side can take a walk; and you're well-advised to assume that it just might happen.

Of course, if your adversary could be relied upon to provide a clear warning before pulling out, you could wait until then to seek authority for the higher price (you know, the price the client previously told you "wasn't in the cards"). But you can't really be sure just when your adversary will abort the negotiations and cut a deal with a third party. He may have given undue credence to your "hard line" (hoist by your own petard!), figured prospects for a deal were dead, and then just failed to show up one day — with no second chance. No matter how you slice it, the downside risk usually exists.

SELECTING AN INITIAL BID

Let's play this out in terms of a specific situation. Remember the dialogue at the outset: you represent the potential purchaser of property, who wants to buy the property for $10 million, which he has also characterized as his top price.

Assume that the seller has other options. Further assume that word has drifted back to you, through intermediaries, that unless your client is willing to *start* the bidding at $10 million, don't even bother coming around. This is the kind of signal that sellers often send — sometimes in fanciful terms such as "eight figures" or "a number with a '1' in front." You should pay some heed, but it's generally part of the negotiating dance; in most cases, you don't *have* to comply.

I should note, though, that some businessmen in this situation are afraid to bid below $10 million, for fear the seller will get up and walk out of the room. Such buyers usually end up overpaying for properties. If you come in with a reasonable first bid — albeit not quite what the seller would like to see — coupled with good rationale and an indication that you're willing to negotiate, my experience is that very few sellers take a walk; they much prefer to stay around and see what develops.

Selecting a smart initial bid is important. Good lawyers definitely involve themselves in the choice. The client determines what price he wants to pay and how far he's willing to go; but if the lawyer is chief negotiator of the deal, he should mastermind the bargaining process — to which the starting point is basic. And for that purpose, he must know the client's maximum price.

In this case, where your client wants to buy the property for $10 million, it's definitely unwise to start the bidding at that number. You can characterize it as your first and only bid; but even if you ooze sincerity, the other side won't buy it. They'll assume you have something more in your pocket and hold out for that. Negotiators have to feel they've made their adversaries budge — it's almost a psychological necessity. So give yourself some room to manuever, while keeping in mind your client's concern over the seller walking out.

Let's say you decide to make an initial offer of $9 million, with a good story as to why this is a solid bid — it's difficult to justify more for the property on a discounted cash flow analysis; here's why even this bid was a stretch — but suggesting, in ways a savvy seller's lawyer will pick up on, that you're not at your limit.

Well, lo and behold, the other side doesn't walk out or laugh you off the premises. They do, however, explicitly refer to their eight-digit message and promptly counter with a strong $13 million asking price. By strong, I mean the negotiator states that his real price is $15 million, but he's willing to settle for $13 million if your client is prepared to pay all cash and close within a couple of days; or he's looking to sell in the $13 to $15 million range, which you read as a willingness to go to $13 million (although he's provided himself an additional later concession when he agrees to take the bottom of his range).

THAT CRUCIAL SECOND BID

The question you now face is what your next bid should be and — equally as important — how to characterize it. It sounds like there's a deal to be made in the area of $11 million, but your client's stated top is $10 million. You have at least three choices here:

- You could stick at $9 million, term the $13 million proposal "ridiculous," and hope that the other side will bid against itself. This is really playing hardball, though, and given the circumstances outlined (including the seller's other options), it carries a real risk of blowing the deal.

- You could go up to $9.5 million, leaving at least one more move to the $10 million level. This is less risky than sticking, but it deliberately defies the seller's eight-figure precondition (now made explicit), and may put him in a spot where he feels he has to walk away from the table to save face.

- You could go all the way to $10 million, but only in a way that makes the other side believe it's your final bid. For this, you need to muster up all the sincerity at your disposal; otherwise, they'll assume you still have more room. Credibility is so basic to negotiation. You can't say, "This is it," and not mean it; if your bluff is called and you fold, you might as well forget about your bargaining posture on all other aspects of the agreement.

Let's assume your client is nervous, so you bid the $10 million with a tears-in-the-eyes speech. And let's further assume the other side believes you. Now, if they're really willing to do a deal at $10 million, they'll accept — congratulations! But if they're not willing, then they may reject it without making another bid, since you told them it wasn't any use — in which case the deal is dead. (This might happen without your knowledge; you just find out later that the seller went somewhere else.)

On the other hand, the seller may suspect you're not finished bargaining, and so he drops his asking price to, say, $12 million. If you want to maintain the credibility of your position, you'll have to reject this without raising your own number. But that won't bring the two parties together; and your real interest lies in keeping the negotiations going.

IF YOU ONLY KNEW. . .

If the situation were different and your client had told you he was prepared (if need be) to go to $11 million, you

could then make the $10 million bid without characteriz-
ing it as a final offer. It could be dressed up in terms that
suggest moving to this level was sheer agony, but at least
you've signaled the other side that the negotiation is still
alive.

Your real hope then would be that the seller comes
down to between $11 and $12 million, at which point
you're pretty sure you can get the deal done. For instance,
if the seller offers $11.5 million and characterizes it as
splitting the difference (between $10 million and $13
million), then you have a good shot at getting the
property for less than $11 million — the seller's move to
the middle being premature while you're still at the $10
million level (a subject discussed below in the essay
entitled, "The Vegas Resolution"). You can even try to
stay at the $10 million level for one more round after the
seller's move, in order to test his willingness to come
down further — yet without having to characterize it as a
final position.

Often, the last five percent movement in a deal can be
the toughest obstacle — especially where both parties feel
they've gone as far as they're willing to go. To bargain
effectively at this juncture, you have to know what your
leeway is. A client's ostensible (but not real) limits can
really impede his a lawyer's quest for a mutually satisfactory way to bridge that final gap.

GETTING THE CLIENT TO LEVEL WITH YOU

Now, how can a lawyer impress a client with the
importance of taking the lawyer into his confidence? I
suggest a totally candid approach. If you sense that your

client isn't leveling with you, try something along these lines:

> "Look, George, I appreciate the fact that lots of businessmen prefer not to tell their lawyers what their actual top price is — afraid of giving away the store, the old self-fulfilling prophecy idea." [Note: You didn't single him out, or call him a liar, but instead placed him in good company.]

> "But, you should know, that's *not* the basis I operate on. If you tell me your real limit, and I don't make a better deal than that, I won't feel I've done a topnotch job. My goal is to shoot for your *desired* number, or even to better it." [Note: Here you've shown that you're on his side, not like those other make-a-deal-at-any-price yokels.]

> "The fact is, though, that negotiations don't always go according to plan. Sometimes the other side won't budge and, if you want the property, you're forced to approach your limit."

> "Now, in order to advise you on the proper starting bid for these negotiations — a price well below what you'd like to buy the property for — and how best to characterize that bid, and in order to figure out what to do as the negotiations progress, I need to know how far you're willing to reach." [Explain reasons why.]

> "And so, George, let me ask you again, what's your maximum price?"

If that's too heavy for you, there's a more jocular approach – in effect, "I know the game you're playing, George, and I don't want to deprive you of your fun, but if you'd just throw me a wink to show there's a little more room, I'll know how to handle the negotiations." It's what might be termed *implicit* leeway, which is often all you need.

If the client doesn't level with you on the first round (even following such a speech), that doesn't mean you can't go back later, after the negotiations have gone on a while, to see if there's been a change of heart. Tell the client where the situation stands and how you intend to handle it, on the assumption there are no more dollars. Show him how this may not work, and in fact could lose the deal for him. Tell him how you would handle it if you had a little kicker, and explain why this gives you a better chance of being able to make a deal. Then, let him decide whether to provide the extra room. You may be pleasantly surprised at the results.

A TURBULENT DECADE FOR DEALS: ANATOMY OF A MERGER REVISITED

[In 1975, I authored a book about doing negotiated acquisitions, entitled Anatomy of a Merger.[1] *In 1985, I wrote this article, spotlighting the myriad ways in which the practice had changed during the subsequent decade. I've made a few further modifications to the article prior to this re-publication, in order to reflect the current state of the art.]*

*   *   *

In 1975, when *Anatomy of a Merger* was published, the world of mergers and acquisitions was relatively straightforward.

THE GOOD OLD DICHOTOMOUS DAYS

On the one hand, there were friendly acquisitions, accomplished through lengthy negotiations in a time-honored fashion that hadn't varied much over the years. It didn't even matter too much whether the company being acquired was privately-owned or publicly-traded; and

---

[1] J. Freund, *Anatomy of a Merger: Strategies and Techniques for Negotiating Corporate Acquisitions* (Law Journal Seminars-Press, 1975) (hereinafter cited as *Anatomy*).

since most of the issues discussed in the book were equally applicable to both types, I generally focused on the private company acquisition, where it was easier to get a sense of the negotiating process. Oh, sure, there were *some* distinctions — the purchaser couldn't seek indemnification from the stockholders of a public seller; a proxy statement was needed when the seller was publicly-held — but the deals got done in basically the same way: a one-step, merger-type transaction that, upon approval by the seller's board of directors and a majority vote of the stockholders, bound all stockholders.

At the other end of the spectrum were hostile takeovers of public companies, a phenomenon which in 1975 had already gained considerable notoriety — although nothing like the situation existing a decade later. Back then, unfriendly takeovers were completely antithetical to friendly transactions, in that there was no opportunity for meaningful negotiations between the parties. The aggressor, rejected in its attempt to strike a deal (or foregoing what would be a futile gesture), went over the heads of the target's board and management, straight to its stockholders. The vehicle was a tender offer which, if successful, resulted in the raider owning sufficient shares to control the target. Once that was accomplished, the target's directors were usually replaced by the raider's nominees, with the target eventually being merged into a subsidiary of the raider.

In 1975, these two worlds were so far removed from each other that I was able to get through 134 pages of *Anatomy* without even a mention of hostile takeovers — at which point, I declared that

> "the objectives, the analysis, the negotiating strategy and tactics peculiar to contested situations are so at variance with their counterparts in the typical

friendly acquisition that the subject [is] beyond the scope of this book.''

THE HOSTILE-FRIENDLY CONTINUUM

Well, that kind of distancing is no longer possible. If I were writing *Anatomy* today, it might well resemble two separate books. The material on acquiring a private company would be very similar to what I wrote in 1975, because the practice hasn't changed all that much; and, in that arena, I consider *Anatomy* to still be quite useful. But entire new sections would be required to deal with the developments of the past decade in terms of acquiring public companies.

Don't get me wrong; *Anatomy* would still not be *about* hostile takeovers — that remains a separate subject with quite different considerations than those applicable in negotiated acquisitions. But, in today's world, the hostile takeover has permeated the public company acquisition scene to such an extent that the practitioner is literally forced to face up to new ways of accomplishing the parties' goals.

In the first place, it's the hostile takeover (or the destabilizing threat of its imminence) that so often motivates companies, not previously disposed to being acquired, to negotiate a deal — either with the potential aggressor on the best terms available, or with a so-called "white knight" who arrives on the scene to rescue the beleaguered target.

Moreover, the former dichotomy between hostile takeover and negotiated acquisition has developed into much more of a continuum, with deals sprinkled all along the line. How, for instance, would you characterize various forms of the "bearhug" approach — ranging up to the unilateral public announcement by the purchaser of a "friendly" offer to merge — by which an acquiror seeks to gain its target's attention? Or, what term would you use to describe the shotgun merger negotiated with a bidder who, two weeks earlier, commenced its unsolicited tender offer by an ad in *The Wall Street Journal* — with the litigators preparing precautionary briefs in the next room right up to the moment of closing?

As contested deals proliferated and gained relative respectability, investment bankers and lawyers borrowed techniques honed in the hostile arena to accomplish negotiated transactions — techniques utilizing such potent, time-condensed methods of proceeding as block purchases and tender offers.

OTHER CONTRIBUTING FACTORS

There are several other related factors — crystallized by the hostile takeover surge, though not totally dependent on it — which contribute to the overall picture. Heading the list is the tremendous hunger for desirable acquisition candidates. It's clear that American business would rather buy than build; good companies are in great demand. Wall Street's investment banking firms have stoked this fire masterfully — initiating many of the approaches, scrambling around for white knights, validating the bidding contests; and most recently, they've started playing a merchant banker role, utilizing their own funds to purchase or finance the property. While in 1975 it was possible to do a deal without the intervention of investment bankers, in today's souped-up acquisition scene they're a ubiquitous and permanent part of the landscape.

The gentility which formerly characterized much of the American business community is now in relative tatters. To be sure, there remain plenty of companies which eschew outrightly hostile acquisitions — if not always on policy grounds, then at least for such practical reasons as the higher risk of inheriting a sullen (or disappearing) management team. But many of these purchasers have less hesitation over applying other forms of pressure (such as the "bearhug" approach) to persuade recalcitrant managements to negotiate with them. And once a third-party deal is announced (the target having thereby shown its willingness to be bought), these "friendly" purchasers rarely feel constrained from poaching — dangling a higher bid to try to filch the deal from the prospective acquiror.

The boards of directors (and even the managements) of target companies have, over the years, become much more aware of their fiduciary responsibilities to stockholders. That doesn't mean they're required to negotiate the sale of the company just because someone comes along waving a fistful of greenbacks. But, there's less ignoring of the realities; and, for the most part, once the company is definitely "in play," directors try to get the best deal possible for their stockholders.

Finally, this decade has witnessed the startling emergence of leveraged buy-outs. No longer is a well-heeled corporate purchaser requisite; when a company (or division) is up for sale, an investor group can be formed to buy it, utilizing the company's own cash, assets and cash flow to generate the funds and service the debt. In fact, in many deals today, the apparent corporate buyer is really just a beard for the real party in interest — the investment banking firm or banking institution that is raising or supplying the funds to make the deal possible.

A TURNING OUTWARD

It all comes down to this: a decade ago, in doing public negotiated deals, our entire attention was directed inwardly. Purchasers and their lawyers worried about whether they were getting the full scoop on the seller through adequate representations and warranties — about whether they had created sufficient covenants to hold the seller constant for several months until the deal was consummated — about whether the requisite conditions to closing were there to enable the purchaser to avoid its obligation if the seller turned out to be less desirable than at first blush. Sellers and their lawyers fretted over reciprocal concerns, such as whether the purchaser would try to wriggle out of the deal down the road. It was all so *insular;* we ignored the rest of the world.

But today, merging parties and their counsel spend as much time worrying about what's going on "out there" as "in here." Everyone realizes (except, perhaps, the Texas judiciary!) that no deal is done until it's done — that even the existence of a seemingly binding agreement doesn't guarantee immunity from assault. And that becomes the focal point of the purchaser's interest; indeed, where the seller is desirous of merging with *this* purchaser (as contrasted with some actual or potential raider), it's also the *seller's* overriding concern. And, what with the hunger for acquisitions, the aggressiveness of major companies and their advisors, the lack of respect for pending deals, the presence of big investor money, and the fiduciary responsibilities of target boards, there's no wonder —

It's a jungle out there!

So, how do lawyers (and others charged with getting deals done) operate today in the public acquisition area? In a nutshell, they negotiate in private in order to arrive at a point where, when the world finds out something's happening, it's as close to a done deal as possible — with the undone parts getting taken care of posthaste. Put another way, the overriding goal of the parties is to make it very tough for anyone to crash the party.

This all began in the late '70's. By 1979, as I found myself increasingly pointed in this direction, using some new techniques (in rudimentary form) and noticing others doing the same, I wrote an article with Rich Easton in *The Business Lawyer,* entitled "The Three-Piece Suitor: An Alternative Approach to Negotiated Corporate Acquisitions."[2] It was clear then that this *modus operandi* was catching fire. In the years since, as the techniques have become increasingly honed, the fire has become a conflagration, and the methodology a basic, permanent part of the acquisition scene.

THE CURRENT TECHNIQUE

If you cut through the welter of mechanics, there are basically three key aspects to the current technique, each of which contrasts sharply with prior practice. (Let's first assume, for these purposes, that we're dealing with an all-cash deal — leaving the complexities of stock and hybrid deals to be discussed below.)

Binding Agreement. Nowadays, the parties make every effort to negotiate straight through to a binding merger agreement — not merely a non-binding agreement in principle — before any public announcement is made. Although a merger agreement may not be ironclad, it's certainly a major step in the direction of finality. Once an agreement is signed, walking away from the deal or

---

[2] 34 *The Business Lawyer* 1679 (July, 1979) (hereinafter cited as *Suitor*). My thanks also to Rich Easton for his helpful suggestions in connection with the present article.

attempting to renegotiate isn't so easy. And the merger agreement furnishes the basis for steps 2 and 3.

Moreover, today's merger agreements contain some provisions with real teeth. The acquired company is invariably asked to agree not to solicit, cooperate with, or furnish confidential information to a competing bidder (the so-called "no shopping" clause). And even *corporate* purchasers are demanding sizeable "bust-up" fees should their deal be topped or they otherwise lose out on the prize — fees initially designed to compensate leveraged buyout specialists for serving a stalking horse function to pry loose sweetened offers from third parties.

This quest for definitiveness contrasts sharply with former practice, in which a public announcement went out the minute the parties' minds met, or at least upon signing an agreement in principle or letter of intent — in any event, at a point when neither party was bound. In today's world, that would be open season for anyone wishing to steal or sabotage the deal.

Lock-ups. Since the merger agreement by itself doesn't always guarantee success, the purchaser also attempts to "lock up" the deal through whatever means is available. This usually involves gaining control over large amounts of the seller's stock. If, for instance, some big blocks are held by insiders, the purchaser will contract with the holders to buy the shares.[3] Since the price is the same as is being paid in the merger, the seller usually doesn't care whether his shares are bought under the contract, in the

---

[3] When this practice was developing, it was typical for the blockholder's shares to be purchased outright at this point. The appearance of the Hart-Scott-Rodino Act (discussed below), which in sizeable deals precludes consummation of the stock purchase until expiration of the applicable waiting period, has altered this practice. *Suitor,* p. 1697. Today, the typical contract with the blockholder is very tight, with no conditions to closing other than Hart-Scott-Rodino clearance.

tender offer (see below) or as part of the merger.[4] The seller generally agrees to vote the shares in favor of this merger transaction and against all others.[5] And, most importantly, no competitor for control of the target can get his hands on the block.

Where no big block exists, the purchaser might consider an open-market buying program to build up his initial stake. Buying stock without the seller's knowledge, however, is inadvisable, as it usually engenders real hostility when disclosed after the fact. If asked for permission in advance, the seller will generally insist that the parties first negotiate, sign and announce their merger agreement. (As you might imagine, the idea of the purchaser gobbling up shares at market prices considerably lower than the value of the unannounced deal, while not yet committed to merge, is anathema to the seller — not to mention the fact that a vigorous buying program runs up the market price and thus reduces the apparent premium being offered, to everyone's dismay.) In any event, since the Hart-Scott-Rodino Act applies to open-market purchases, there are strict limits on how much stock can be accumulated in this manner prior to making

---

[4] Sometimes, however, tax considerations or concern about short-swing profits under Section 16(b) of the Securities Exchange Act of 1934 make one form of disposition more desirable than the others. In addition, a well-advised blockholder will seek "price protection" in any such contract, to ensure that he gets no less through this avenue than the purchaser is paying other stockholders in the merger or tender offer. There may be room for negotiation here; see *Suitor,* p. 1707.

[5] Be careful not to go too far here, though. If all the indicia of ownership (such as the right to receive dividends and vote the shares) become the purchaser's, this could be deemed a change in beneficial ownership prior to the running of the Hart-Scott-Rodino waiting period.

the necessary filings and observing the prescribed waiting period.[6]

Nowadays, as a *quid pro quo* for the full price he's willing to pay in the deal, the buyer generally asks for (and gets) an option from the seller corporation on large quantities of its authorized but unissued (or treasury) common shares. A frequent measure is 18-1/2% of the previously outstanding shares,[7] which is the largest size deal that doesn't require shareholder approval under the rules of the New York Stock Exchange. The purchase price of shares under the option is most often the same as the merger price, although buyers often negotiate — with occasional success — to have the option exercisable at or near the market price for seller's shares just prior to announcement of the merger agreement, or at some price in between. The buyer doesn't intend to actually exercise this option; rather, it's viewed as a deterrent to others — plus a means of assuring the buyer a tidy profit if a third party successfully tops his deal.

By contrast, a decade ago we rarely dealt with outstanding shares on a piecemeal basis. Certainly, the idea of taking an option on shares from the selling company — a tactic originating as an inducement to white knights to join the fray against a determined hostile bidder, but now routine even where no raider exists — was not even contemplated.

As if a right to buy stock from the target wasn't enough, close on its heels came the so-called "crown jewel" option. This device — which would have generated shocked disbelief in years past — enables the purchaser,

---

[6] The investment exemption under the Act, permitting purchases of 10% or less of the target's stock, can't be relied on when a merger is in the offing.

[7] Note that, on a fully distributed basis, this works out to roughly a 15.6% stake in the target company.

in the event someone successfully jumps his bid, to buy a particularly desirable segment of the seller's business at an attractive price. The intended effect, of course, is to discourage others from making a run at the company, since what they'll end up with (if they succeed) will be minus a crucial part. This tactic also originated as an inducement to reluctant white knights, but in recent years has sometimes been used in the first instance. Crown jewels have had some rough sledding in the courts, however;[8] and I'd be loathe to recommend one unless the merger price represents a substantial hike over what might otherwise be available, the fairness of the amount payable for the crown jewel has been blessed by the seller's independent financial advisor, the board has followed a careful decision-making process, and the deck isn't stacked in favor of a management-sponsored bidder.

Tender Offer. Most cash merger agreements today provide that the purchaser will immediately initiate a cash tender offer for any and all shares of the seller, at the price being paid in the merger. No waiting around for the merger to take place, with the inevitable delays of preparing a proxy statement, shepherding it through the SEC, soliciting stockholders to vote at a special meeting — the tender offer gets the job done faster and more effectively. And it's expressly sanctioned by the merger agreement and recommended by the seller's board.

By the time the purchaser gets around to completing the merger itself, it's pretty much of a formality — since the purchaser has by then become the owner (and voter) of the bulk of the seller's shares.[9] This last step may have

---

[8] See, e.g., *Revlon v. MacAndrews & Forbes Holdings, Inc.,* 506 A. 2d 173 (Del. 1986).

[9] Outstanding shares held under lock-up options can either be tendered into the purchaser's tender offer or bought separately *after* termination of the tender offer — SEC Rule 10b-13 prohibiting any such purchase while the tender offer is in progress.

the look of a "going private" cash merger, but in actuality it's an integral part of a unitary acquisition plan — no more of a freeze-out than occurs to shareholders who vote against a single-step merger.[10]

ANNOUNCING A "DONE DEAL"

The object of all this is to be able to put out a strong initial public announcement — contrasting sharply with the traditional statement that the parties had reached an agreement in principle — along the following lines:

> "Purchaser and Seller announced today the signing of a definitive merger agreement for the acquisition of Seller by Purchaser.

> "Under the agreement, approved by the boards of directors of both parties, Purchaser will commence tomorrow a cash tender offer for any and all shares of Seller's common stock at $20 per share net, to be followed by a cash merger at the same price.

> "The S family, which owns 25% of Seller, has granted Purchaser an option to buy its block at $20 per share. In addition, Seller has granted Purchaser an option to buy 1,000,000 authorized but unissued shares (about 18-1/2% of Seller's outstanding shares) at $20 per share."

You can see how forceful this is.

- Purchaser already owns, in effect, 25% of the Seller's stock.

---

[10] See discussion of the final-step merger at pp. 1718-23 of *Suitor.*

- If someone challenges the deal, Purchaser can get its hands on another 18-1/2%, which amounts to control for all practical purposes.

- There's a signed merger agreement, approved by Seller's board, which contains powerful "no shopping" provisions designed to block access to Seller by interested third parties and impede the flow of information in that direction.

- Purchaser is commencing a tender offer tomorrow, and in 20 business days will probably own over 90% of Seller's stock, either obviating any vote on the final merger or making it merely a formality.[11]

That's the goal practitioners strive for today.

PRO'S AND CON'S OF MULTI-STEP DEALS

The principal advantage of using block purchases and tender offers to accomplish negotiated deals is that the purchaser gains control of the seller faster. Time is precious here; the quicker control shifts, the more likely the deal is to happen, the less likely any competing bids will surface. The price paid for that advantage is the reduced opportunity for a full-scale purchaser's investigation and a diminution of the traditional plethora of contractual protections — considerations which take a back seat when the bargaining occurs under real pressure of time and secrecy. On balance, most (but not all)

---

[11] Many states permit so-called "short-form mergers," by board action alone, when a high percentage of stock is owned by the parent. See, e.g., Del. Gen. Corp. Law § 253 (90%).

36

acquisition-minded players today take on the risks of the multi-step deal.

It's not simple, however, and there are numerous hurdles and complexities along the way—tender offer rules, Hart-Scott-Rodino waiting periods, Stock Exchange limitations, and so on. But the toughest aspect — and one that has come under increasing scrutiny by the Securities and Exchange Commission — is to make it through to signing a definitive agreement without being forced (by leaks, rumors, the seller's share price running up on big volume, the Stock Exchange's pointed inquiries) to make a premature announcement — the bane of all professionals charged with insuring the success of a deal.

THE PRESSURE TO MOVE SWIFTLY

The effect of these circumstances is to put great pressure on lawyers and others involved in the process to negotiate quickly and quietly; to forego kicking tires and taking other due diligence measures that were commonplace in the old days, for fear of letting the cat out of the bag; and to use stripped-down forms of agreement, with many fewer old-fashioned lawyer's protective provisions and much more reliance on the accuracy and completeness of public filings, tempered by the informed judgment of practical businessmen.

That's one of the big differences today from a decade ago. Large corporations are increasingly willing to make acquisitions of public companies based primarily on the public record. People have come to trust these filings — the occasional horror story of widespread fraud being comparable to the news of an airplane crash, which rarely deters other travelers.

And, if he has his priorities straight, a few days of intensive scrutiny, aided by a cooperative seller, can resolve most of the major questions a prudent buyer might have. Let's face it, the extensive representations and warranties drawn up by lawyers — Is the seller qualified to do business in Utah? Are the insurance policies properly scheduled? — rarely deal with the essential quality of the product or the future of the business. When he has only a couple of days, the buyer has to concentrate on the gut issues — understanding the market, recognizing the need for capital expenditures, becoming comfortable with the projections. (The projections are particularly crucial; when they prove to be both positive and credible, the white knight who sees them can often outbid the hostile raider who hasn't had access.)

Negotiating styles are also changing to suit the times. Lawyers and others charged with doing deals have learned to put matters more in perspective — to look for compromise solutions, rather than standing pat in hopes that a long siege will bring the other side around. There's far less fancy footwork when you get only one shot at doing it right.

Moreover, in the old days, when the time lag between signing and closing the merger was lengthy,[12] the conditions precedent to the purchaser's obligation to close were critical. Nowadays, where the bulk of the target's shares are bought and paid for within a month, the conditions to the mop-up merger are far less critical — since by then, the purchaser has paid out the bulk of his investment and is unlikely to leave the last step unfinished. The real negotiations should take place over the

---

[12] Deals were often conditioned, for example, on receipt of a tax ruling, which typically took many months to pry out of the Internal Revenue Service. Today, it's much more typical for the parties to rely on a tax opinion from the seller's outside counsel.

conditions to the *tender offer* — the takedown of shares being the point at which the purchaser has to put up the big money. The classic "conditions" section of a tender offer, spawned in the unilateral hostile mode, contains an out for almost anything adverse that might happen — and purchasers' lawyers, drafting friendly tender offer deals, often start off with just that kind of provision. The key for sellers' lawyers here is to whittle the conditions down sufficiently so that, once the deal is signed and announced, the purchaser is really committed — even more so than in an old-fashioned one-step merger. Then, once shares are bought under the tender offer (or lock-up options are exercised), the purchaser should be bound to close, come hell or high water.

One delightful by-product of all this is the decreased dependence on legal opinions in multi-step, stripped-down acquisitions. The old nightmare of holding up a deal your client really wants because you're unable (for technical reasons) to deliver a required opinion, is much less prevalent today.[13]

HYBRID TRANSACTIONS

Up to now, we've been talking mostly about all cash deals. Once the use of purchaser's *stock* enters the picture, things become more complex. Tender offers don't work

---

[13] It's interesting, though, that in some two-step deals where legal opinions are still sought at the time of the merger, purchasers typically don't ask for such opinions at the time the preceding friendly tender offer closes — which is really the moment when that particular brand of assurance would seem most welcome. This is an example of legal practice not quite catching up to events — we still tend to think of tenders as unilateral transactions, in which the purchaser has no one to rely on but himself.

with paper; exchange offers utilizing shares or debentures face delays, uncertainties and (in some cases) substantial tax and accounting risks. This is why all-stock deals, no matter how attractive, have trouble competing with cash acquisitions.

A major change in the '80's has been the increased use of hybrid forms of purchase price, with a little of this and a little of that: cash, common stock, preferred stock, debentures. The most typical configuration is roughly half cash, half common stock. For the stockholders of the seller, there's a choice; and while cash is generally more popular, those who wish to defer taxes might opt for the purchaser's stock. From the purchaser's point of view, an all cash deal might be too expensive — creating too much debt, or weakening the companies' combined financial position — while using all stock might be too dilutive, so the combination works best.

The usual pattern in a 50-50 deal is for the parties to enter into a merger agreement which provides for the seller's stockholders to receive purchaser's common stock in the merger, but which also calls for a 50% cash tender offer by the purchaser up front — the idea being that, by the 20th business day after the tender offer commences,[14] the purchaser gains effective control of the seller, even if it still takes several months to complete the merger. Moreover, the shares purchased in the tender offer are voted by the purchaser in favor of the merger, making its approval a virtual sure thing.

The combination of two- or three-step deals (block purchase, tender offer, mop-up merger) and two kinds of consideration leads to exquisite complexities. And don't believe for a moment that these matters are neutral from a

---

[14] The tender offer, by law, must commence within five business days after it's announced. The announcement — unless forced prematurely — is made when the merger agreement is signed.

negotiating standpoint. Take a question like whether to do that 50-50 deal with a tender offer first, or simply as a cash election merger (where stockholders send in their proxy and check the box for cash or stock). Technical point, huh? Forget it. Quite different consequences can flow for each side, depending on which format is used and how the stock is valued.

For example, the purchaser probably wants to have a cash tender first, to maximize the cash element and gain effective control of the seller earlier. The seller may well agree, particularly if being acquired by *this* purchaser is desirable (since the tender makes this deal more certain); on the other hand, the seller runs at least a theoretical risk of the second step not being completed and having to live with a new controlling stockholder — leading sometimes to never wholly satisfactory negotiations over contingent "standstill" provisions.

With respect to the stock element of the merger, the *buyer* might well prefer to base the ratio on stock values at the time the agreement is signed (e.g., two shares of buyer's stock for one share of seller's), in order to know the maximum dilution in advance. The *seller,* on the other hand, will worry that if (as usually happens upon announcement of the deal) his shares go up and the buyer's shares go down, a fixed exchange ratio will be worth less to the seller's shareholders than the cash portion of the price. So, the seller might rather base the exchange ratio on stock prices over a period closer to the time of the merger. But the potential dilution to the *buyer* here (should his shares decline in value) makes the buyer uncomfortable enough to insist on a so-called "collar" (i.e., no matter how much his stock drops, he won't have to issue more than 2.2 shares for each seller's share). This, in turn, forces the *seller* to seek a collar on the other side (no fewer than 1.8 shares under any circumstances); and that leads to a discussion of rights to terminate the deal if the stock price falls below or rises above the collar — and we're off to the races.

Just to make things more difficult, there's no law that says the value of the stock in the back end has to equal the cash price in the tender offer. In hostile deals, so-called "front-end loading" of offers — say, pricing the tender offer at $40 per share, with securities valued at $35 to be issued in the merger — is sometimes used to put maximum pressure on stockholders to tender or sell to arbitrageurs. While few friendly deals start out with this kind of disparity, it can still happen when the friendly acquiror or white knight finds himself in a bidding contest with a raider; and then there's even more pressure placed on the lawyers, who are trying to be fair to everyone.[15]

REGULATORY ASPECTS

A pervasive element of public deals today, as contrasted with a decade ago, is the presence of a host of regulations that didn't exist or weren't applicable back then.

The Hart-Scott-Rodino Act, for example, requires the closing of sizeable acquisitions to be deferred for specific periods of time while the Justice Department or Federal Trade Commission takes a look at the anti-trust aspects of the deal. The mandatory waiting periods — which apply in different ways to block purchases, tender offers and the

---

[15] Since all stockholders are offered the higher tender price, there's no discrimination about this kind of front-end load — just a nagging fear that sleepy or ill-advised holders won't get in on the tender and will thus receive the lower merger price for all their shares, while the market professionals will take maximum advantage of the price disparity by tendering everything they can get their hands on.

merger itself — can affect strategic decisions and present an additional negotiating variable to take into account.[16]

Tender offers are regulated under specific SEC rules that emerged in the hostile process and aren't always suited to friendly deals.[17] For instance, where a tender offer is part of a negotiated transaction, it must begin within five days after it's announced — which puts great pressure on the lawyers and everyone else concerned. It does result in a lot of information coming into public hands quickly (as contrasted with the usual wait of several months before a merger proxy statement surfaces publicly). On the other hand, in a negotiated cash tender for any-and-all shares (other than one which qualifies as a "going private" transaction), there may be less information provided about the seller than is included in a cash merger proxy statement — including the absence of material undisclosed facts (regarding, for example, under-valued assets) — simply because the purchaser doesn't have knowledge of them.[18] And in that two-step hybrid transaction, there is little significant information about the resulting company provided to the seller's stockholders in the tender offer materials, which is the critical time when they must make the decision whether to tender or wait for the merger.

Nevertheless, the SEC has made substantial progress in the '80's toward implementing its integrated disclosure system. For example, the Form S-4 we now use slims

---

[16] For Hart-Scott-Rodino issues, see *Suitor* pp. 1697-1700; and see generally, Axinn, Fogg & Stoll, Acquisitions Under the Hart-Scott-Rodino Antitrust Improvements Act (1979).

[17] See Freund and Greene, "Substance Over Form S-14: A Proposal to Reform SEC Regulations of Negotiated Acquisitions," 36 *The Business Lawyer,* 1483 (July, 1981).

[18] This may be rectified, to some extent at least, in the Schedule 14D-9 which the seller is required to send to its stockholders within 10 business days after a tender offer commences.

down the bulky package formerly distributed to stock-holders in merger-type transactions involving the is-suance of securities, primarily through incorporation by reference to other filed documents for company-related information.

AN ACQUISITION IS STILL A DEAL

If I were writing *Anatomy* today, this would be one of my themes: that amid all this complexity — the welter of SEC regulation, the mechanics of tenders, the complica-tions of multi-step deals, the investment banking aspects of hybrid consideration — and the pressure to move ahead while simultaneously building barriers against third party intrusion, it's easy for lawyers and others involved in the process to lose sight of the fact that an acquisition is still a deal between two parties. That shouldn't be allowed to happen — because the particular point where the parties end up striking a deal is still, in large part, a function of how well they bargain.

Not totally, of course; the bargaining leverage is more often tilted today. [See the following article, "When the Playing Field Tilts."] A beleaguered seller, under siege by an undesirable hostile bidder, may not be in a position to hold out for much when the only white knight available agrees to come to the rescue at the eleventh hour. The knight understands this and bargains accordingly, hang-ing tough at all the significant places. Conversely, a desirable target can create almost an auction-like atmo-sphere, dictating the terms and conditions of its acquisi-tion — and many purchasers will go along, since the particular terms may be less important than winning the prize.

But there's still room for creative negotiating by lawyers who realize that very little is neutral in deal work and speak up at the right time. It's trickier than it used to be, though:

- You really have to rack your brain to envisage all the ways things can go wrong.

- You should have a feel for the financial aspects of the deal, as well as the dynamics of market activity and tender offers.

- With litigation often a factor, you need a sense of what tactics courts will sanction and where they draw the line.

PRIVATE COMPANY ACQUISITIONS

Now, what about acquisitions of privately-owned corporations? I happen to think that the decade-old material in *Anatomy of a Merger* is still directly responsive to the concerns of lawyers representing buyers and sellers of private companies.

To be sure, changes have occurred in some of the rules and practice, although most of these are more in the nature of nuance than real substance. Purchasers worry today about sellers' ERISA compliance, unfunded pension liabilities and environmental problems; there's been some tinkering with the Internal Revenue Code (for example, it's easier now to get installment treatment in an earn-out deal); and registration rights are less difficult to negotiate, with the simplified registration procedures now in place.

We've also seen some spillover from the public arena. In *Anatomy,* I advised purchasers of private companies to announce the deal early — even before the parties were bound — so as to put the seller at a negotiating disadvantage (the idea being that the latter couldn't risk *not* closing and face the inevitable assumption by his peers that the buyer had unearthed some skeleton in the seller's closet). I don't give that advice today, with all the poaching that goes on. If no announcement is required on materiality grounds, I try to go right through to closing before breathing a whisper of the deal — or, at least make sure there's a binding agreement in place, obligating the key stockholders personally.

But most things haven't changed. We still use those long-form contracts, since there are no public filings to rely on (sometimes, not even reliable financial statements) and we're seeking gobs of information in a formal manner with legal consequences — most significantly, to make sure that the purchaser is held harmless if, down the road, he discovers he's been had. So, *Anatomy*'s "Four Horsemen" analysis of representations, covenants, conditions and indemnification still applies in spades. The main difference for me — after years of operating principally in the fast-paced world of public deals (both friendly and hostile) — lies in how difficult I now find it to sit for hours at the bargaining table, arguing over insertion of the word "material" in Section 3.2.4. or the phrase "to the best of our knowledge" in the representation on trademarks. . . .

I've learned something else, too. Some of the most difficult negotiations in an acquisition are with your own client. [See the previous article, "Negotiating With Your Own Client".] You can't make a deal without compromise; you can't compromise without movement on both sides; and most movement is toward the center. Getting your own people to cede points, to up the ante — without your being perceived as "giving away the store" — calls for every bit as much skill as slipping one by a distracted adversary.

* * *

And that's the way it is, a turbulent decade later.

WHEN THE PLAYING FIELD TILTS: NEGOTIATING LEVERAGE IN ACQUISITIONS

Seller-1, a private company, is about to run out of funds, at which point a bankruptcy filing will be inevitable. Its investment bankers have canvassed all possibilities, but the only prospective purchaser of the company is Buyer-1. Unfortunately, Buyer-1 realizes it has no competition. Negotiations are about to begin between the parties; you represent Seller-1. . . .

* * *

Seller-2, a public company, owns certain related properties that it wishes to sell. Because each property is individually desirable (although the aggregate might not appeal to a single purchaser), the investment bankers have advised Seller-2 that the best way to maximize the price to is to conduct separate auctions for each of the properties. Under that method, the investment bankers have estimated that Seller-2 will net between $90 to $100 million (and possibly somewhat more) from the sales. Two days after public announcement of the planned auctions, Buyer-2 informs Seller-2 of its strong desire to purchase all of the properties as a unit. Seller-2 advises Buyer-2 that, based on what it expects to net from the auctions, it will consider selling the lot only if Buyer-2 makes a preemptive bid in excess of $100 million and enters into a hell-or-high-water agreement ensuring that the deal will take place. You represent Seller-2 as the negotiations commence. . . .

* * *

49

Buyer-3 has commenced a unilateral tender offer for any and all shares of Seller-3, a public company. The price is not a full one, but sufficiently above market that Buyer-3 will acquire control unless shareholders are presented with an alternative. Though its investment bankers scour the landscape for a white knight, Seller-3 fails to interest anyone in joining the fray. Buyer-3, aware of the search, suspects that Seller-3 has been unsuccessful. Finally, three days before shares can be purchased in the tender, Seller-3 approaches Buyer-3 to try to negotiate the best deal possible. The approach at this late hour confirms Buyer-3's suspicions as to the lack of competition. You represent Seller-3 in the ensuing negotiations. . . .

*   *   *

A hostile bidder has made a unilateral tender offer for Seller-4 which will clearly carry the day if no better deal can be found. Seller-4 has a low opinion of the bidder and will do almost anything to stay out of its clutches. Litigation, a possible leveraged buyout, restructuring proposals — ultimately, none of these provides a way out. A few days before the tender offer is to be consummated, the desperate search of Seller-4's investment bankers finally bears fruit — Buyer-4, a tolerable white knight, surfaces. At these prices, however, the deal is only marginal for Buyer-4, and its management is decidedly risk-averse. You represent Seller-4 as the negotiations with Buyer-4 begin. . . .

*   *   *

A hostile tender offer has been made for Seller-5 at an inadequate price. Seller-5 would make an extremely desirable acquisition for any number of companies. Its attempts to remain independent fail, and the Seller-5 board of directors puts the company up for sale. Within hours, four of the biggest, richest companies in the industry signal their willingness to engage in a bidding war to win the prize. Seller-5 has no particular preference among the four companies. There is adequate time to complete a deal before shares can be purchased under the tender offer. You represent Seller-5 as negotiations commence with Buyer-5 (one of the four companies) — with each of the other eager bidders waiting its turn in the wings. . . .

*   *   *

What do these five situations have in common? In each case, as counsel to the seller, you are about to commence negotiations with the deck somewhat stacked — either in your favor (as with Sellers 2 and 5) or against you (as with Sellers 1, 3 and 4). But, in the complex universe of mergers and acquisitions, this is by no means uncommon; in fact, the existence of positive or negative leverage is more and more the order of the day.

Rereading today what I wrote years ago about negotiating acquisitions, I'm struck by the implicit assumption that the negotiations take place on a level playing field; *i.e.,* that each party approaches the conference room with the same degree of voluntariness and roughly the same quantum of desire to accomplish the transaction, and that each has a similar willingness, if the significant provisions cannot be worked out to its satisfaction, to walk away from the deal.

Well, that's not a bad academic model to start from in assessing what can be accomplished through bargaining; but as an insight into today's real world of M&A negotiations, the premise is a bit naive. The converse is possibly closer to the facts — namely, that in most deals nowadays, one or the other of the parties has arrived at the table in less voluntary fashion, possesses a stronger desire to achieve a negotiated outcome, and has a greater reluctance to terminate the negotiations unsuccessfully.

Moreover — although here, my personal statistical sample is smaller — I have a sneaking suspicion that

similar disparities also pervade other commercial endeavors. Am I wrong, or isn't it the case that every day, in villages and hamlets throughout the land, lawyers sit down to bargain either holding lay-down hands or caught between a rock and a hard place?

For example, we've all observed how often the two sides have differing inducements for reaching a negotiated resolution to a commercial dispute or active litigation. Plaintiff A revels in the pressure his lawsuit is bringing on Defendant A, a business competitor; as a consequence, Plaintiff A is not really receptive to attempts to resolve the matter, even on terms which are equitable. Plaintiff B, by contrast, has a real need for part of the funds held by Defendant B, which are the subject matter of the dispute; thus, Plaintiff B feels intense pressure to settle early, even at an otherwise unsatisfactory price. Defendant C believes he has much the better of the case, and is willing to put his judgment to the judicial test — causing him to resist settling the litigation for other than a nominal amount which Plaintiff C can't accept. In each of these cases, the parties may be talking, negotiating, seemingly trying to strike a bargain; but their degree of commitment to the process — and consequently, the postures they adopt, the positions they take, and the flexibility they reveal — can vary considerably.

Well, you may ask, so what? Doesn't this just mean that I'm going to cut a better or worse deal than I'd otherwise make? My reply is, no, it means more than that. It means that many of the negotiating principles and tactics applicable to a level playing field aren't well-suited when the field tilts. Lawyers involved in negotiations, who fail to appreciate these dynamics, do so at their clients' peril. Fighting for protections that may otherwise be appropriate but are not in the cards for the under-leveraged side; failing to secure reasonable advantages obtainable by the over-leveraged party; knowing when to stick and when to fold, when to press and when to ease up — all these factors, essential to the effective performance of a negotiator's job, flow from a sense of where the parties stand.

This essay is designed to sensitize lawyers to bargaining leverage — measuring its existence, dealing with *apparent* leverage, coping with weakness, and making the most of a strong posture.

My focus will be on mergers and acquisitions, though many aspects are equally applicable elsewhere. The added twist in M&A, however — and what makes the problems so much more devilish there — is the acquiror's ability to accomplish a hostile takeover against the public seller's wishes, which brings great pressure to bear and infects the entire process.

MEASURING LEVERAGE

Let's begin by trying to isolate the principal factors that create positive or negative leverage in an acquisition bargaining situation. These factors often operate in tandem, exacerbating each other; sometimes, however, they work at cross purposes, creating waves of turbulence as they vie for predominance.

Necessity. The first consideration is whether the seller is being forced to sell. (Instances in which a *buyer* is forced to buy are pretty much limited to those involving a pre-existing contractual commitment, which raises issues outside the scope of this essay.) That, for example, is the plight of Seller-1, on the brink of financial collapse, desperate for a quick sale. Seller-1 might still have been able to exert some leverage if it had been able to find another bidder; but with only Buyer-1 in the game, Seller-1 is in terrible bargaining shape. The alternative of being able to walk away from the table if satisfactory terms can't be negotiated puts backbone into a party's ability to bargain; while, to sit there glued to your seat, afraid to take any step that might terminate the negotiations no matter what pillage your adversary perpetrates — that's an excruciating experience (as I can testify!) which virtually eliminates needed flexibility.

Similar bleak circumstances would exist for the party forced to sell a business by a certain date to comply with a governmental divestiture order — with the date fast approaching and only one buyer interested. And this is what can happen with the hostile takeover, where failure to reach a deal will result in an involuntary change of control. That's the situation faced by Seller-3 (who has only the hostile bidder to negotiate with as the tender offer deadline nears) and by Seller-4 (relegated to negotiating against time with an indifferent white knight who knows he's the only game in town). It's analogous to the negotiations between a prospective defendant and an outraged claimant with a strong case; like the looming threat of successful litigation, the unilateral tender offer hangs over the proceedings like a corporate sword of Damocles.

Desire. Assuming there's no necessity to deal, the next consideration is: who wants the deal *more* and how strongly does he feel about it? [See the later essay entitled, "Who Wants the Deal More?"] To answer this question, you often have to dig beneath all the posturing of the parties — but where real disparity of desire exists, the more relaxed party has a definite advantage in the negotiations. This plays out most graphically on the issue of price, where closure of the gap between the amounts initially bid and asked turns on who's willing to move more (usually the avid party) and who tends to stand firm (Mr. Couldn't-care-less).

So, for example, in the case of a private company seller in good financial condition, it's often the buyer who wants the deal more. The individual controlling the seller may have mixed emotions about parting with "his baby," which results in him taking non-constructive bargaining positions — even becoming mesmerized by his own bloated asking price. For the buyer, by contrast, this might represent a great fit with his other business operations, or a critical new strategic imperative; if so, the buyer may be tempted to pay an exorbitant price to realize "his dream." The leverage could shift the other way, though, if both parties sensed the stirrings of new competitive pressures on the seller's business in the near future, and there's a relatively attractive offer from the buyer sitting (but not indefinitely) on the table.

Competition. The third major consideration is whether or not other potential buyers are vying for the right to acquire the seller. The pressure on the buyer to pay a rich price multiplies when competition for the seller exists; at the same time, the presence of other bidders stiffens the seller's resolve to hold out for top dollar. That's the environment for Seller-5 and its four salivating suitors. The same factor can also be used by a seller *before* the bidding begins, as illustrated by the conditions Seller-2 imposed on Buyer-2 to preempt its intended auction. And the *absence* of such competition, as we've seen, can be deadly to the bargaining posture of a seller who is forced to make a deal.

Time. Finally, there's the pressure of time, which cuts across each of the other factors. A party acting under a deadline (which doesn't impact the other party) often makes decisions and takes actions, at variance with its conduct under more relaxed circumstances, which play right into its adversary's hands. On the other hand, if other leverage factors are operating in its favor, the party under the time pressure can sometimes use this to advantage — forcing the other side into an earlier decision than otherwise desirable.

To my mind, these constitute the major leverage factors operating in a deal context. That's not to say there aren't others — for example, a frequent consideration of no small significance is whether some executive's prestige is on the line, tied to the successful completion of the deal. Non-acquisition bargaining situations, of course, have their own leverage factors. (For instance, A and B are parties to an ongoing agreement which has some time to run and hasn't been breached. For business reasons, A wants to revise certain terms in the agreement; B prefers the status quo. The deck starts out being stacked in B's favor.) And we've seen some of the unbalancing considerations in resolving disputes or settling litigation — who's holding the money or property, who has the stronger legal or equitable position, who is more advantaged (or disadvantaged) by the continuance of the litigation.

For our purposes, though, we'll concentrate on the Big Four — Necessity, Desire, Competition and Time. The ways in which these four factors interact — in one situation, all pointing in one direction; in another, tending to neutralize each other — can often determine the outcome of the negotiations.

THE APPEARANCE OF LEVERAGE

Exerting leverage in negotiations (or having it exerted against you) is not just a matter of the *actual* leverage that the parties do or don't possess, but also depends on the *appearance* of leverage to the respective sides. Mistaken impressions as to your own strength or weakness or that of your opponent can definitely affect the bottom line.

Overestimating your own strength or underestimating that of your adversary causes many a deal to be blown; while, to overestimate an adversary's strength or underestimate your own often results in too high a price being paid (or too low a price accepted).

So, when you get involved in a negotiation, it's wise to take these steps:

1. Try to accurately gauge your own strength or weakness;
   — If your position is strong, make sure this is adequately communicated to your adversary;
   — If your position is weak, do your best to keep the other side from realizing this;

2. Attempt to gauge the other side's actual strength or weakness;

3. Decide whether your adversary's perception of his strength or weakness is in accord with reality;
   — If your adversary thinks he's stronger than he actually is, educate him to the real facts;
   — If your adversary thinks he's weaker than he actually is, *DON'T SAY A WORD!*

This is an important role for the lawyer-negotiator to play, not only in terms of dealing with his counterpart on the other side, but also in orchestrating a total effort by all the players on his own team — executives, investment bankers, etc. — in order to transmit a consistent message to the adversary. Nothing is worse than, having gone to great pains to get a message across to your opposite number, finding out you've been undercut by, for instance, an uninformed utterance from your client's press spokesman.

Communicating strength where it really does exist might seem a simple exercise, but it presents two problems. The first is that you're just not believed. In a game of poker, which is a classic win-lose situation, having your opponent read your actual strength as merely a bluff can be terrific — he stays in the game and you end up raking in the sweetened pot. But in negotiating agreements, where a win-win outcome is required (in the sense that each party has to be sufficiently satisfied with the results to sign the contract), to possess the strength, but have your opponent think you're bluffing and act accordingly, may be the worst of all worlds.

So, your first objective is to achieve credibility (which is a subject for an article all to itself). I would only say, in passing, that two of the key ingredients are consistency in the message you deliver — e.g., as the moment of truth nears, you can't suddenly elevate to the status of a deal-breaker a point which you treated casually in the earlier rounds — and resisting the temptation to overstate your case (overstatement being the common refuge of the bluffer and perceived as such by an astute adversary).

The second problem in communicating strength is that you come across as so smug, so arrogant, so overbearing, that your opponents — by now, completely turned off — take retaliatory actions that might not be in their most rational interest. Don't let this happen. Communicate your strength quietly, in a non-arrogant manner, letting the position speak for itself and keeping personalities out of the way. Don't be confrontational, causing your adversary to bluff or harden a position, which will reduce flexibility later on; just let the facts sink in, not calling for a response, but influencing the other side's deliberations in the quiet of their caucus. (Your chances of getting the other side to bow, scrape and congratulate you publicly on the strength of your position roughly equate to the likelihood of a real-life defendant confessing on the stand *à la* Perry Mason.)

Now, communicating strength when it *doesn't* exist is, as you might expect, a much tougher job. For a lawyer, the difficulty is heightened by his reluctance to lie, dissemble, mislead — all the traditional tools utilized by bargainers to accomplish this task!

But his reluctance is well-placed. It's not just that the canons preclude a lawyer from asserting as a transactional fact anything that he knows isn't true or can't reasonably be inferred from the available information. And it's not just that a lawyer who consistently misrepresents facts gains a reputation for untrustworthiness that can be harmful to his career. It's also that lying is antithetical to everything we lawyers should care about — everything that elevates our profession above the morals of the marketplace. [See the later essay, "Lying in Negotiations".]

On the other hand, nothing in the canons requires you to acknowledge your client's weakness or to reveal the inner workings of your mind. And you can certainly try to eliminate overt signs of the pressure or desire your client feels. This goes beyond masking a sweaty brow or ruling out anxiety-ridden glances at a wristwatch. Focus, for example, on the president of your buyer client, who starts out as a salesman, trying to convince the seller to throw in his lot with the buyer. The trick here is — once the seller is over the hump — to get the president acting as a negotiator; otherwise, the more he overtly salivates at the prospect of the seller joining the fold, the more the seller is encouraged to stick with his unreasonably high asking price.

A recurring concern here is the dilemma faced by the seller and his lawyer, attempting to negotiate with the bidder against the backdrop of a hostile offer, when the seller has no alternative bid from a third party. The more the bidder (such as Buyer-3) is convinced the seller has no alternative, the harder line the bidder is inclined to take.

Only if the bidder is concerned that his tender offer might be defeated by an alternative transaction can the seller cut a decent deal.

It's a tough situation — take it from someone who's been there more than once. The first rule is, try to keep it from happening. Even if another deal is unlikely, have other irons in the fire which the bidder can't completely ignore. If no other companies are interested, then develop alternative transactions — a leveraged buyout, a restructuring offering competitive values to shareholders, and so forth. Finally, if you're concerned whether any other options will eventuate, and you bear no animus against the bidder, you might decide to approach your opposite number *early* (time, as usual, is the key here), with the proposal that he consider making a preemptive bid before you open the bidding to all comers.

What you *can't* do is to invent something that doesn't exist — creating another offer out of whole cloth to use as leverage. Still, you're not required to tell your adversary that you lack alternatives; and should he ask, there are a number of ways to block or avoid the direct question without resorting to lying (e.g., "I'm not going to open my client's kimono for your benefit. . ."). Nor must you behave as if you had no other options — the last time I looked, the canons contained no proscription against keeping up a bold front.

YOUR BACK TO THE WALL

Now, let's examine the situation where you're at a clear bargaining disadvantage and both sides know it. Does this mean you're completely without resources in the forthcoming negotiations? Not at all. But it does mean that, after educating your client as to the realities of life, you should define and aim at certain limited objectives — distinguishing between what's achievable and what's not.

This distinction does *not* mean that important things are not achievable (although, to be sure, many things aren't) and all you can hope for are some crumbs. Rather, the distinction turns on whether the issue is, on the one hand, either essentially arbitrary or subject to differing rational conclusions — as, for instance, price — in which cases, the odds are clearly against you; or, on the other hand, either handled relatively uniformly in deal practice or subject to one outcome that is clearly the most rational result, in which cases, you've got a fighting chance.

With essentially arbitrary issues, you're unlikely to make much progress. And on points having alternative resolutions that are equally equitable, your batting average won't lead the league. But, many of the issues discussed in an acquisition are common to most deals, and, over time, certain established outcomes — falling within a relatively narrow range — have come to be accepted as the norm. There's no reason why you shouldn't exert some effort to end up within acceptable limits on these points. Moreover, where your arguments in justification of a point are logical and unanswered, there's a good chance you'll ultimately prevail. You may lack clout in terms of power, but your leverage here is to wrap yourself in the mantle of "conventional practice" and "reasonableness" and hope that your adversary will prove to be fair-minded.

This isn't as unlikely as a cynic might suspect. Most of the attorneys who ply this trade find themselves, from week to week, on different sides of the fence. Any tendency for a lawyer to overreach when positioned on high is offset by the knowledge that next month he may be down looking up — and would then appreciate receiving the same professional courtesy that you're seeking from him today. I find that most lawyers representing the strong position are receptive to appeals made on a reasonableness or customary usage basis; and while this doesn't guarantee that they'll promptly cave in, few practitioners force you into a completely untenable position.

Take a situation like the one existing between Seller-2 and Buyer-2. Given its willingness to auction off the properties separately in the absence of a preemptive bid, Seller-2 is indeed in a strong — although by no means impregnable — bargaining position. If Seller-2 sticks to its unwillingness to discuss a purchase price below $100 million, Buyer-2 is unlikely to be able to dislodge Seller-2 on this issue. But let's look at three other issues that might arise in the bargaining.

Suppose that, unlike the usual situation (where the purchaser prepares the acquisition agreement), the seller hands the buyer the form of agreement it intends to distribute to all bidders in the auction. (Seller-5, conducting its own quasi-auction with four eager bidders, might take the same tack). The draft:

- contains virtually no representations on the part of seller;

- does not prohibit seller from soliciting other purchasers for the properties even after the definitive agreement is signed; and

- provides that the only basis on which the buyer can terminate the deal is if a material adverse change in seller's business has occurred between signing or closing, or if the discrepancy between what has been represented and what's true is materially adverse to seller's business, financial condition, or results of operations.

Buyer's lawyer objects. On the first point, he argues, Buyer-2 can't buy a pig in a poke. But, he's willing to focus the representations on the financial statements of the subsidiary in which the properties reside — and not get into all that stuff about due qualification in remote states and the terms of minor leases. The precedents, he says, are overwhelming; in almost every deal anyone has seen, the seller has at least represented the fair presentation of its financial statements. Well, it's hard for Seller-2's lawyer — no matter how strong he feels his client's position is — to argue against what's been done everywhere else (including, if Buyer-2's lawyer is sharp enough to point it out, specific deals in which Seller-2's lawyer represented other unpressured sellers!).

On the no-shopping point, Buyer-2's lawyer doesn't even bother arguing precedent (although he might well have). He just says, "Hey, come on, we're paying this preemptive price to go to the head of the line, in front of everyone else. We can't have you out there trying to hustle someone else into interfering with our contractual rights after we sign. . . ." and so on. The lawyer for Seller-2 has no logical retort; his adversary is entitled to this provision and he'll get it.

On the third point, however, no matter how Buyer-2's lawyer kicks and screams, Seller-2 is likely to prevail. Admittedly, the hell-or-high-water terms sought aren't inevitable (although they're not unusual) in the deal world; plenty of transactions are signed which permit the purchaser to terminate upon the failure of matters having far less consequence. But here, where Seller-2 is giving up the auction route for Buyer-2's preemptive bid, the seller's attorney wants to know that the deal won't come unglued at a later point. With logic backing that position, my bet is that if Buyer-2 wants the deal, he'll eventually fold his tent on this one.

There's a style point here worth briefly noting. If you're the beleaguered counsel, the one sure way to guarantee that your well-positioned adversary will feel no compunction about nailing you to the wall is if you come on in a shrill, hectoring style. This is *not* the time to try to throw your weight around (though the frustration at your powerlessness may lure you in that direction). You're attempting to appeal to reason; such appeals are best handled in a reasonable manner, with each request accompanied by carefully considered rationale. That's not to say your points should be wrapped in apologetic tones or presented weakly — just the opposite, since the quiet self-assurance of an unassailable position is about all you've got going for you.

When, notwithstanding your exemplary efforts, you get turned down on one of these points (which you will!), and you've exhausted your appeals, then, assuming the point is not a deal-breaker, it's best to give in — not on the principle but to the power. Your attitude should be, okay, I won't prolong the agony on this point; but buddy, you owe me one! — hoping that some tremor of remorse might cast its shadow across your adversary's brow when the next meritorious issue comes to the fore.

The toughest moments to handle, when the leverage is overwhelmingly against you, are naked displays of power by the other side — a buyer dropping its price, a seller reneging on concessions previously granted, anyone suffering a convenient loss of memory or taking a totally irrational position. There is a great desire — left over from other deals where your client had this luxury — to tell your adversary to "get lost." But you really must control your emotion, bite your tongue, and attempt to work up a strategy to deal with the situation. Maybe there's some fat in his proposal, at least around the edges, that can be eliminated from the final product. Perhaps you can revive something you lost on an earlier round as a swap for the new item — particularly when there's a logical tie-in between the two. But if your client has to do this deal, then you must be constructive — don't let yourself become part of the problem rather than part of the resolution.

That's not to say, however, that you shouldn't let your opposite number understand just how foully you view this depredation. Keeping the moral and equitable pressure on — even when your big guns (the ability to pack up your yellow pads and walk out) are spiked — may eventually yield some deserving dividends.

IN THE DRIVER'S SEAT

Now, I'd like to switch to the opposite situation — when it's *your* client that's in the driver's seat.

For a purchaser's lawyer, the real power stems from those situations we've just looked at — where the seller is backed against the bankruptcy wall, or your client's hostile tender is on the brink of success, or you represent the only available white knight to rescue the seller from a hated hostile bidder. When you're the legal right arm of Buyer-1, Buyer-3 or Buyer-4, you can afford to hang tough. (I say "you" because, for some inequitable reason I can't fathom, I rarely seem to get one of those choice assignments; more often, I'm near the ground, looking up. . . .)

I would hope, though, that if I had the good fortune to be negotiating from such strength, I'd behave reasonably, treating my adversary with the kind of professional courtesy previously referred to. Life's too short for crusades, retribution, power games, and associated junk.

Here's how I think a responsible lawyer who happens to hold all the cards ought to behave. On issues where your client is immovable, indicate your position to the other side in quiet but unequivocal terms — just so no one is operating under the delusion that there's room to negotiate. (This may seem hard-nosed, but it's in everyone's best interests and saves a lot of frustration down the road.) Express some rationale for each position, to avoid being seen as totally arbitrary. Don't cut off your adversary's requests, arguments, rebuttals — even if they're fruitless; he'll want to be able to tell his client he raised these points, albeit to no avail. Finally, don't insist on winning everything; couple the issues on which you're unbending with others of less significance on which you accept at least part of your adversary's argument, so that he's not made to feel totally helpless.

Viewed from a seller's perspective, the clearest case of maximum negotiating leverage is what Seller-5 faces — where two or more willing and able suitors are simultaneously vying for the prize, and the seller doesn't care which camp he ends up in. (I stress "simultaneously" because, were this to occur sequentially, it becomes much tougher for the seller to know what to do — whether to take the good bird in the hand or wait for the possibly great bird in the bush; and I stress being unconcerned about who is the eventual buyer because, if the seller *does* care, then there's a wholly different dynamic at work.)

This is a delightful situation for a lawyer to find himself or herself in; and in today's active acquisition climate, it's not an unusual state of affairs — even for me! The seller would generally prefer that each buyer know the other is there — spurring them on, in the true spirit of the auction, to bid boldly against each other and augment seller's bottom line. And, rest assured, this setup can cause the competitive juices to flow, sometimes resulting in a purchaser whose reach far exceeds his grasp.

Turning for the moment to Buyer-5's side of the equation, this is precisely the situation in which he doesn't want to find himself. As a result, some buyers try to make exclusive dealing the keynote of their willingness to up the ante. Here's the standard speech: "Look, I can make a big bucks bid here; but if I do and you shop it, then you can consider it withdrawn." This is designed to put the seller — who knows there's another bidder out there, but not how high he's willing to go — in a tough spot.

Of course, there's a real difference between "shopping a bid" and the seller's ability to deal with other buyers. At the first buyer's insistence, the seller can promise not to reveal the amount of his bid to another buyer, or even (if it hasn't been publicly disclosed) the first buyer's identity. But the seller can then still go to the second buyer and say, "I have a strong bid from a real buyer, the identity and terms of which I can't reveal to you — except to say that if you don't do better than where you're at now, we're likely to go with him. So put your best price on the table; you only get one shot."

When the seller is a public company, it's hard for the buyer to completely tie the seller's hands — since once the company is clearly up for sale, the courts have emphasized the seller's obligation to strike the best deal for its stockholders. Then, too, not every bidder who says, "If you talk to anyone else, my bid disappears," is believed; there's a certain credibility problem in making that proposition stick.

From the point of view of the seller's lawyer, bustling from room to room negotiating with several buyers, the bargaining over issues other than price — issues in which the lawyer tends to play a key role — can be very enjoyable. There should, however, be a certain delicacy to the exercise. The buyers don't like the position they find themselves in, and you don't help your cause by rubbing their noses in it any more than necessary. Nevertheless, whenever one of the buyers (but not the others) takes a hard-line position on an issue that's important to the seller, here's what I like to say (as seller's counsel):

> "Look, the seller's board is going to make the ultimate decision between the different deals based solely on the merits. Obviously, price is paramount; but other considerations may be important also. My goal, as attorney for the seller, is to be able to present the board with as level a playing field as possible in terms of these other issues. Your competitors have *not* insisted on this point. I suggest you see your way clear to doing the same, because otherwise you may lose the deal even if your dollar bid is as good as any on the table — since the principle at stake is an important one to the board."

This is a particularly useful strategy when the issue involves a legal point, since the last thing in the world the buyer's lawyer wants to see happen is for him to lose the deal for his client by insisting on protections that may not really be needed. Even on a business issue, it works well — particularly against an insecure executive of the buyer, who doesn't want his boss to think he's blown the deal. But remember, you can't use this too much, or it loses its force; save it for the main stuff.

By the way, when you're representing a seller in the driver's seat, be sure to do your negotiating over the terms of the agreement *while* the auction is still in progress. Once the seller selects one suitor over the others — and assuming the prospective buyer knows he's won the contest — the leverage can shift very abruptly. This is particularly true if the winner has prevailed by paying a helluva price — all of a sudden, by God, he thinks he deserves some contractual protection! — and your client isn't about to risk letting him off the hook over some "lawyer's point."

How about that other setup — where the seller prefers one of the buyers over the others? This can be a tricky situation; much of the leverage enjoyed by a seller who's indifferent to the winner's identity is dissipated when a clear preference emerges. The key here is somehow to ensure that the bid of the favored buyer ends up at least in the same ballpark as the competition. What's the best way to make that happen?

Well, ordinarily in negotiations, it's not such a good idea to let your adversary know that you favor him or his product, since this might tempt the adversary not to extend himself in the bargaining. In this area, however, my sense of the psychological imperative at work is that it's important to advise the favored bidder of his status — coupled with a more-in-sorrow-than-in-anger warning. It usually runs something like this:

> "Look, we *want* to end up with you; we can see a great future together for our companies *[here, you sell a little. . . .],* but you're making it awfully tough by sticking at this price, which your competition has already exceeded. We're willing to do what's needed to end up with you; but, if you *really* want us (as you say you do), you've got to stretch a little. . . ."

*   *   *

Well, I could go on at length about the joys of being on top (or, for that matter, the agony of the gutter), but I think it's evident that considerations of leverage have to affect the negotiator's attitude and posture at every turn.

Now, if someone could please tell me how I can land as clients a few of those high-riders so I can climb out of this consistent hole, I'd really appreciate it. . . .

THE ACQUISITION MATING DANCE

With all the emphasis today on hostile takeovers and corporate greenmail practitioners, the more subtle (but no less fascinating) developments on the negotiated-merger scene — particularly, the cat-and-mouse choreography of today's acquisition mating dance — have generally been overlooked.

Here's the basic situation. On one side, there's a target company ("Target") whose stock trades on the American Stock Exchange at a modest multiple of earnings and a hefty discount from book. It's a tempting plum for some larger, acquisition-minded company to go after. (If the cash flow is ample and the capital spending needs moderate, Target will also attract attention from the financial players on the takeover scene — but that's a subject for another day.) However, Target's chief executive officer ("Mr. T") has a long-range corporate plan that he needs time to implement, so he's in no mood to be acquired just now.

On the other side, there's a big company out there ("Acquiror") which would love to acquire Target. Acquiror's chief executive officer ("Mr. A") has long had designs on Target's principal business, which is closely related to Acquiror's core operation. "What a great fit Target would be!" Mr. A has been known to exclaim to his senior advisors. And Acquiror is sitting with plenty of cash, plus a stock selling on the New York Stock Exchange at a healthy multiple — enabling it to pay a handsome price for Target, either in cash or stock or a combination of the two.

Now, like other executives in similar situations, Messrs. T and A operate under certain legal, ethical, and practical guidelines that impose limits on their total freedom of action — guidelines that reflect the attitudes of their respective boards of directors. Mr. T, for his part, understands that he owes a fiduciary duty to the stockholders of Target. If a really attractive offer were to be made for the company, he would feel obliged to give it serious consideration. Still, he hopes never to be placed in that position, and will do what he can (within the limits of propriety) to avoid its occurrence.

Mr. A, for his part, is unwilling to initiate a totally hostile takeover. In common with many American businessmen, he doesn't believe in forcing another company to be acquired against its will. His view is not solely a matter of principle, but is grounded in such practical considerations as the following:

- Hostile acquisitions are less likely to succeed than negotiated ones; even if the target ends up being acquired, it may be by someone else (a so-called "white knight");

- The litigation accompanying a takeover is always expensive, can be messy, and may even prove embarrassing;

- If a bidding contest develops, the initial bidder — its reputation on the line — may end up paying too much in order to win the prize;

- Once a company has initiated a single hostile takeover, future targets will disbelieve its protestations of friendship;

- The use of force can result in acquiring a sullen, dispirited management — if, indeed, the top executives stick around at all — which may not bode well for future operations.

On the other hand, Mr. A understands that he may need to employ certain means of exerting pressure short of an outright raid to get the attention of desirable acquisition candidates, so many of whom (like Target) seem committed to remaining independent.

I represent corporations that resemble both Target and Acquiror, and I have advised a number of chief executive officers who think like Messrs. T and A. In recent years, I've become fascinated by the highly stylized maneuverings that mark this type of corporate courtship. Like the Charleston Rag in the 1920's or World War II's Lindy Hop, the Acquisition Two-Step of the 1980's is very much a product of its time. The movements are subtle; the zigs and zags legion; the outcome, rarely preordained. The players may be uncomfortable with the roles they're called upon to perform — roles that can be at odds with their business personalities. It's easy to err, and missteps can be fatal.

But that's enough characterization (and probably too much metaphor). In order to analyze the issues involved, let's examine some actual proceedings — the possible approaches, the range of responses, effective countermeasures — placing ourselves alternately in the positions of Mr. T and Mr. A, together with their advisors.

THE INITIAL APPROACH

We'll start with Mr. A. He's a realist — he suspects that Mr. T will not be thrilled at the prospect of Target being acquired. And since Acquiror won't invoke the ultimate

sanction of a hostile takeover, Mr. A has to interest Mr. T in making a deal. How to do it?

Well, like many chief executive officers, Mr. A thinks his best shot is to talk directly to Mr. T. Chances are, Mr. A considers himself a persuasive man — after all, he didn't rise to the top at Acquiror without some skills at salesmanship — capable of convincing Mr. T how desirable a combination of the two companies would be.

Mr. A's concern, however, is that he'll be rejected by Mr. T out of hand, with no chance to tell his story. Word has it that Mr. T has brushed aside other suitors in the past; is there any reason to expect a warmer reception today? (In some cases, especially when the two companies share a common industry, the chief executives already know each other; in fact, Mr. T may actually have spurned Mr. A's prior feelers a few years back.)

So, Mr. A spends hours with his advisers, fussing about the initial approach to Target. How about writing a letter? No, says Mr. A, that's too cold and formalistic — it's just not my style. (I must say that I agree with Mr. A; and since the letter lacks the key ingredient of his salesmanship, it's unlikely to generate a positive response.)

How about an indirect approach? There are various oblique ways to make the first contact with Target. One of Acquiror's outside directors may be friendly with a counterpart on Target's board; perhaps he could conduct some initial soundings to see if there's any interest. Or Acquiror's financial adviser might contact his opposite number at Target's investment banking firm to try to drum up a little business.

But indirection doesn't suit Mr. A's style, either; he didn't get where he is by relying on others to do his dirty work. And since he reads Mr. T as the kind of executive who dislikes being circumvented by an end run, Mr. A is concerned that such probings would evoke a negative response, which might prove difficult to overcome.

So, Mr. A determines to make the first contact with Mr. T himself, directly, by means of a telephone call, in which he will suggest that the two of them get together for a chat.

A POLICY OF INDEPENDENCE

Now, let's switch over to Mr. T. At this point, though he's unaware of Acquiror's imminent approach, he knows that Target would make an attractive acquisition for a number of large companies. And Mr. T has sought counsel on his responsibilities from a lawyer experienced in the field, who has advised as follows.

Mr. T and his board have a fiduciary duty to duly consider any bona fide offer made for Target. But if, in the board's judgment, the best interests of the stockholders would be served by first molding Target into a stronger and more effective company — so that any sale would occur down the road, when Target's goals had been achieved and it could command an acquisition price approaching its real worth — well, then Target can pursue a policy of remaining independent until these developments actually happen. Since this is exactly the way Mr. T and his board feel about the company, they have adopted a policy of independence.

That policy has shaped Mr. T's reaction to merger-minded approaches. According to his lawyers, Mr. T is under no obligation to sit down and discuss the acquisition of Target with anyone who pops into town seeking a meeting. Likewise, he is not obligated to try to convert preliminary feelers into a firm offer. If an offer is made that the board and its advisers consider inadequate, he need not negotiate for improved terms, or search around for a better bid, or declare an auction, or otherwise put the company up for sale.

DECLINING INVITATIONS

Mr. T's legal and financial advisers also have given him some sound practical advice. If you want to pursue a policy of independence, they have said, then be careful not to let yourself get into compromising situations — such as accepting an invitation to sit down with a potential purchaser to discuss acquisition. The problem with most American businessmen, according to Mr. T's lawyer, is that "they're too damned polite." When a fellow chief executive invites them to lunch, they're inclined to accept the invitation; and that can spell trouble.

I agree with that advice. People in the acquisition business, who are accustomed to being told to "get lost," seize on any ray of hope that suggests a willing seller. In this climate of wishful thinking, a target's willingness to meet may be viewed as a highly favorable sign.

(These same cockeyed optimists construe a response of "no interest" as, "I think he might well be interested," based on a non-negative tone of voice. Replies along the lines of, "Well, I'll listen to what you have to say, but we're not for sale," are interpreted as genuine curiosity. And, "I recognize the fiduciary duty we have to our stockholders," is taken as nothing short of, "He definitely wants to do business." My advice to clients is to stop being so polite and — if you're really negative — say "No! No! No!" in unmistakable tones.)

This advice bothers Mr. T. He has always considered himself to be open-minded, dedicated to assessing what is good for his stockholders. How will I know, he asks his advisers, that a specific acquisition proposal *isn't* beneficial for Target stockholders, until I hear it?

Well, say his advisers, this acquisition business is different from other spheres in which you operate. It's a jungle out there. Once someone — even mistakenly — gets the notion that a company is interested in being acquired, the next thing you know a written offer shows up on your desk. At that point, the company will almost certainly be, in the sports-flavored argot of Wall Street, "in play." Tremendous momentum can build up — fueled by arbitrageurs and others who now have a stake in seeing that a deal (*any* deal!) gets done — momentum that may prove impossible to control.

SLIPPING PAST THE DEFENSES

Turning back to Mr. A, you can now see what he's worried about — getting the cold shoulder from a "well-advised" Mr. T. And so, Mr. A's thoughts naturally turn to slipping past Mr. T's defenses — to getting Mr. T into a room without having revealed that the real purpose of the visit is to discuss acquisition. What's unfortunate, though, about this aspect of the mating dance is the strong temptation to dissemble.

The ideal situation, from Mr. A's viewpoint, is for him to call and ask for the meeting without stating its purpose, and for Mr. T to agree to meet without asking what's on the agenda. Unfortunately, that's unlikely to happen, given Mr. T's general level of anxiety and the threat posed by a company like Acquiror. If Mr. A offers no substantive reason for the get-together — "I happen to be coming over to your neck of the woods next Tuesday; how about getting together for lunch?" — Mr. T might well ask,

"What's on your mind?" So, Mr. A has to be prepared to offer a basis for the meeting.

The typical chief executive in Mr. A's position would rather not say, "I want to discuss Acquiror buying Target." It's too direct, too unvarnished — and it invites a response such as, "We're not interested in being acquired, so there's no point in our meeting."

At the other extreme, most chief executives don't like to misrepresent the facts — as, for example, by stating that the meeting is for a completely different purpose. ("I want to talk to you about the proposed new tax legislation, which could impact both our companies adversely.") The idea of lying doesn't sit well with Mr. A; and he worries that when Mr. T finds out what he's *really* up to, Mr. T will be mad as hell at being euchred into lunch under false pretenses.

Still, some businessmen do use this method. If they're successful in getting the meeting, they start things off on the topic of taxes, touch on several other non-controversial subjects, and then finally get around to the idea of acquisition ("Oh, by the way. . . ."). This isn't a technique for amateurs, though; unless handled flawlessly, it's too easy to see through.

Moreover, there's another significant problem with this approach. In order to convey credibility that the merger was indeed an "afterthought," the purchaser's musings on the subject have to be presented in fairly imprecise, offhand fashion. This detracts from the sense he wants to convey (as we'll see later) of a well-thought-out, artfully scripted plan that has an aura of inevitability. You can't pull that tax legislation stunt and then whip out four single-spaced pages of acquisition proposal.

In order to avoid the extremes of total candor and abject misrepresentation, many executives favor using a general phrase which is broad enough to cover the subject of acquisition — such as "I'd like to talk to you about some important matters of mutual interest" — hoping that they won't be asked in advance for greater precision. If pressed for details, they might respond somewhat coyly. ("It's not something that's appropriate to discuss on the telephone, but I'm sure you'll find it extremely interesting.") If pressured further — and fearful that, on such a mysterious basis, they won't be granted an audience — these executives usually level and tell their opposite number what it's all about.

One topic that purchasers often like to use as a lead-in is the possibility of the two companies engaging in a joint venture. This is a prime feint to obtain a meeting. The subject is potentially beneficial to the companies involved, without appearing particularly ominous. Moreover, there's a smooth, rational transition from the subject of joint venture to that of merger — it can almost seem a natural outgrowth of the discussion. In fact, if the listener's interest in the joint venture guarantees a second meeting, the topic of acquisition need not even be mentioned at the first get-together. (I find, however, that most executives figure they'll get only one chance to make their pitch — which makes them reluctant to save acquisition for a later session that might never occur.)

THE COLD SHOULDER

Now, let's examine this from Mr. T's perspective. He receives a phone call out of the blue, from a Mr. A whom he barely knows, suggesting a meeting. My strong advice to Mr. T is to find out the subject of the meeting *before* agreeing to meet. Don't accept the invitation without any statement of purpose from Mr. A, or on the basis of a euphemistic characterization. Press for specifics, regardless of whether that strikes you as impolite. You're a busy man, with lots of commitments; you're entitled to know the real reason for the meeting, in order to decide whether to oblige.

Let's say that, in the course of the phone call, Mr. A reveals to Mr. T (either voluntarily or in response to the latter's queries) that the purpose of the meeting is to discuss acquisition. If Mr. T doesn't want to encourage Mr. A, he should probably reply along the following lines:

> "I'm sorry, Mr. A, but Target is not for sale. Our board and management are committed to a policy of remaining independent, which we consider the best means available at this time to maximize value for our shareholders. There's no point in meeting to discuss the subject, since we're just not interested."

That might sound like pretty stern stuff — and taking such a dogmatic stand bothers some executives — but at least it communicates, clearly and not subject to misinterpretation, just where Mr. T stands.

In the same vein, if Mr. A proffers a specific, non-threatening purpose over the phone, and then at the meeting switches the subject to acquisition, I would advise Mr. T to interrupt immediately, remind Mr. A of his stated agenda, and emphatically rule the acquisition discussion out of order. ("I didn't come here to discuss that; I wouldn't have met with you if I knew that was on your mind; and if you insist on pursuing that subject, this meeting is at an end.") After all, Mr. T has cause to rise up in righteous indignation — he's been snookered into meeting under false pretenses — and he might as well make the most of it.

I find, however, that it doesn't sit well for many chief executives to end a meeting prematurely, and on this sour note. Their tendency is to be courteous to other chief executives, even those with questionable motives — to hear them out. (Among other things, Mr. T may simply be curious to find out what price Mr. A will offer. . . .) But businessmen have to understand that the very act of listening — once the subject matter is known — will invariably be deemed a sign of encouragement in the post mortem session between Mr. A and his advisers; and that can only lead to trouble.

THE ACQUIROR'S LEVERAGE

All right. Let's assume Mr. T greets Mr. A's mention of acquisition (either in the phone call or at the meeting) with an emphatically negative response. How should Mr. A handle the situation? Well, this brings us around to the subject of what leverage, if any, Acquiror can bring to bear on Target.

The stark reality of the situation is that if Mr. A makes an acquisition proposal in private to Mr. T, who rejects it out of hand, and then nothing more happens, that proposal is dead. This, in fact, is just what frequently occurs. And the more Mr. T believes that his outright rejection will cause Acquiror to quietly disappear, the more he'll be tempted to take that route. So, what can Acquiror do, short of an overtly hostile tender offer for Target's shares, to put pressure on Target — at least enough pressure to cause the merger proposal to be given due consideration?

Clearly, Acquiror exerts its strongest pressure by making a firm written offer to acquire Target, containing specifics as to price and other basic terms — a so-called "bear-hug" letter. Now, this kind of proposal differs from a hostile tender offer in one important particular. A tender offer is made by the purchaser directly to the stockholders of the target company, seeking to buy their individual shareholdings; there's no need for any corporate action, either by the target's board of directors (other than making a recommendation on the offer, which, even if negative, doesn't preclude its consummation) or by the target's stockholders acting as a body. By contrast, the bear-hug letter envisions acquisition of the target company by means of a merger-type transaction, requiring in the first instance the approval of the target's board of directors, and thereafter the affirmative vote of the target's stockholders at a meeting called for that purpose.

The pressure arises because, under federal securities law, the receipt of a firm proposal of this nature — containing a price per share that constitutes a healthy premium over Target's current market price — has to be publicly disclosed. From Target's viewpoint, it's clearly a material development; it may also be material to Acquiror, depending on the relative size of the deal.

Even if the deal isn't material to it, Acquiror may announce its delivery of the proposal without waiting for Target to do so. The rationale is to generate a positive tone to the first press reports of the potential deal — including a quote from Mr. A as to how desirable this marriage would be for both companies and their stockholders — as contrasted with the negative vibes that would undoubtedly emanate from a Target press release. When called by the press, Target may not even be in a position to comment on Acquiror's announcement; a knee-jerk negative reaction, prior to appropriate screening of the proposal by Target's board and its financial/legal advisers, is not usually considered advisable.

The purpose in forcing public disclosure of the offer is to start the pressures of the market working, in order to put Target in an uncomfortable position. Many of Target's stockholders will want to be able to take advantage of the premium price being offered; but unlike the case with a unilateral tender offer, they won't be able to avail themselves of Acquiror's merger proposal if Target's board turns it down. So, one hope is that Target's stockholders will bring pressure to bear on Target's management and board to accept (or at least negotiate) the Acquiror proposition.

If "the Street" believes that Acquiror's offer will either be accepted (perhaps on a sweetened basis), or trigger the appearance of other suitors at even higher prices, then arbitrageurs and other market professionals will begin to buy Target's shares, pushing the price of its stock upward and creating unstable accumulations. These blocks of shares — purchased at prices higher than the stock's trading range prior to disclosure of the proposal (and presumably higher than the price to which the stock would sink if Target rejected Acquiror and nothing else surfaced) — are now in hands where they must be sold quickly at a profit. (Such blocks are obviously more volatile than shares owned for 20 years by a retired schoolteacher, resting snugly in the safe deposit box next to the deed for the cemetery plot.) As a result of this activity, Target may well find itself "in play;" and while Acquiror may not end up as the successful buyer, Target's chances of remaining independent will rapidly diminish.

At a minimum, once the announcement is made, Mr. T can't sweep the whole thing under the rug, hoping it will just go away. He has to deal with the proposal — which is precisely what Mr. A wanted him to do in the first place.

The problem with this bear-hug approach, however, is that it's rarely well-received by Target's management and board of directors. In fact, it engenders almost the same sense of betrayal as accompanies an outrightly hostile tender offer — particularly when the news hits the tape (via Acquiror's press release) just about the time that the messenger is delivering the envelope to Mr. T. Once that public announcement is made, it's quite difficult to convene a negotiating session in a cordial, businesslike atmosphere.

In practice, what generally happens is that Target immediately reaches for his investment banker and lawyer — the former to render an opinion (if he can) that the price being offered is inadequate, the latter to opine (if possible) that the combination would be illegal and or to consider initiating legal action designed to keep the deal from happening. And these first reactions can make it difficult to change course later on and work out a deal. It's not just a question of losing face, though this often enters into the question. Positions initially taken — such as the judgment of Target's lawyers that the takeover violates the antitrust laws — can prove embarrassing if the acquisition ultimately gets on track and the parties have to jointly convince the Justice Department that the combination is not illegal.

THE PARADOX OF PRESSURE

Now, in between (a) the private oral proposal that, if rejected, self-destructs and (b) the publicly announced firm written proposal that applies maximum pressure, are a number of approaches designed to gain more leverage than under (a), while not terminating any possibility of friendly negotiations as with (b). For example, a letter that proposes the concept of acqusition, but doesn't state a price, is generally not a disclosable event — since price is so basic to any deal. Other possibilities include letters that:

- State a range of values, the lowest of which exceeds Target's current market price;

- Propose a specific price, but go on to say that, although Mr. A is prepared to recommend it, the proposal has not yet been approved by Acquiror's board of directors and is subject to its assent;

- Contain a price but expressly condition everything on receiving confidential data from Target that supports the price being proposed.

The paradox here — and what makes the maneuvering tricky — is that the more pressure that's exerted, the less likely the proposal will be swept under the rug, but the more likely it will engender a hostile reaction. Conversely, less pressure leads to greater receptivity, but also to an increased likelihood that the proposal will never see the light of day. So, the ideal mix for Mr. A, who hopes to get a negotiation going, is to generate enough potential pressure so that Mr. T can't ignore him, but not so much that Mr. T stops talking and starts to fight.

The central decision in all this is whether or not to put the proposal in writing. Letters create more pressure, but (precisely for that reason) are not warmly received. So, I find that most friendly bidders prefer to start without a writing, although they're apt to have a letter in reserve if they feel the conversational approach isn't getting them anywhere.

THREATS AND COUNTER-THREATS

With that as backdrop, let's return to our basic situation. Mr. A telephones to ask for a meeting; Mr. T probes the purpose; Mr. A is finally forthcoming; and Mr. T says he's not interested in meeting to discuss an acquisition. What should Mr. A do? Well, an effective (albeit somewhat hard-nosed) reply for Mr. A would be along the following lines:

> "I'm sorry you feel that way, Mr. T. But we at Acquiror have done a lot of work on this project and we're quite serious about wanting to pursue the subject with Target. The problem is, if you won't meet with me, I'll be forced to communicate by letter — with a resultant loss of flexibility on both our parts. So wouldn't it make sense for us to get together, so you can hear me out?"

That's strong stuff, calling for a tough decision on Mr. T's part. The last thing Mr. T wants to receive is a letter from Mr. A, which may have the effect of putting Target into play. To be sure, Mr. A could be bluffing — but then again, he might not be. If Mr. T thinks he can turn Mr. A off in a private meeting (but not by ignoring him), then he's probably better off meeting with Mr. A to keep things informal and flexible — perhaps agreeing to meet on the express condition that no letter is handed to him over the hors d'oeuvres. But if Mr. T senses some weakness in Mr. A's armor, then he might want to take a bolder tack — designed to frighten away those who will deal only on a negotiated basis:

> "Look, Mr. A, if you want to make a formal written proposal, I can't stop you. But don't deceive yourself — no matter what hearts and flowers the letter contains, it will not be treated as a friendly overture. So, unless you're ready for a decidedly negative reception, don't even bother to get started."

A LETTER AFTER DESSERT

Now, let's assume a luncheon meeting has been set up to discuss "matters of mutual interest." Just prior to the dessert, Mr. A will raise the subject of acquisition — but not as an afterthought.

Rather, Mr. A's pitch will be that he's been thinking of little else for months. He wants to show Mr. T the seriousness of his intent, in order to suggest the inevitability of the transaction. A casual pass invites quick and easy rejection; Mr. A hopes that Mr. T will feel compelled to deal in businesslike fashion with this more meaningful approach.

In such a context, should Mr. A hand Mr. T a letter or other writing before the meeting ends? (I'm thinking of a letter that states the basic terms of the proposal but isn't sufficiently firm or specific to require disclosure — in fact, it may even state Acquiror's view that no public announcement is required.) Coming to lunch with a prepared letter is definitely a sign of Acquiror's serious intent, and the letter increases the pressure on Target. But delivering a formal writing (even one that begins, "Dear Mr. T") right there and then may upset any fragile sense of camaraderie that emerged during the meeting, throttling any stirrings of interest Mr. T may have felt. Here, from Mr. A's viewpoint, are some other pros and cons of this important decision.

One negative factor is a loss of flexibility in responding to Mr. T's concerns. Let's assume they've had a free-wheeling discussion, during which Mr. T has stressed what would be important to him in the event of an acquisition. A letter prepared prior to the meeting may not address all these issues. It would be better to send the letter the next day, incorporating material that is directly responsive to Mr. T's stated agenda.

On the plus side, if Acquiror's proposal is complex, setting it forth in a writing left with Mr. T is desirable — just to make sure there's no ambiguity or misunderstanding. This doesn't have to take the form of a letter, however; it could consist of a single page setting forth the complex portion.

The principal affirmative reason to deliver the letter (although not necessarily right there at the meeting) is to ensure that Acquiror's proposal will be transmitted by Mr. T to other members of Target's management and particularly to its board of directors. The conventional wisdom for potential purchasers is to get the target's board involved— the hope being that independent directors will respond on the basis of their fiduciary duty to stockholders, even if the chief executive and his management team don't see things quite that way.

Of course, even writing a letter to Mr. T is no guarantee that the proposal will make it to the board. As a result, purchasers sometimes include in the letter a sentence (which is not, as you might expect, universally well-received), along the following lines:

> "In view of the importance of this matter, I know you'll be transmitting this letter to members of your board; so, in order to expedite matters, I'm taking the liberty of hand-delivering a copy to each of the directors."

Now, let's look at the letter issue from Mr. T's point of view. If Mr. T is queasy about being acquired, he should try to discourage Mr. A from leaving a letter or sending one after the meeting. Writings of this kind often take on a life of their own, serving to put Target prematurely into play.

So, at the point in the meeting when Mr. A whips out his letter, I'd advise Mr. T to say:

"No letters, please. If you want to pursue this dialogue on an informal basis, I'm happy to do so; but if you present us with a letter, we're going to treat that as an unfriendly act."

If no letter is proffered but Mr. T suspects one may soon be on its way, he can make a similar precautionary statement at the end of the meeting.

WHAT ARE YOUR INTENTIONS?

What else can Mr. T do, after hearing the proposal? One tactic is to ask Mr. A whether he has hostile intentions. The ultimate threat lurking behind any approach is a unilateral tender offer, and Mr. T would like to know whether it's a realistic possibility. The more likely it is, the greater the odds that Target will end up in play, and thus the more pressure to reach an accommodation. If a hostile tender offer isn't likely, however, then Target has a chance to escape unscathed — which makes it more tempting for Target to discourage Acquiror.

Now, assuming that Mr. A has made the decision not to proceed on a hostile basis, how should he handle this question from Mr. T? If Mr. A foreswears any hostile intentions, then he's putting all his eggs in the "nice guy" basket, which invites a speedy rejection. If he refuses to rule out a takeover, he may have more clout — but Mr. T may also be less inclined to do business with him.

Many chief executives in Mr. A's position evade giving a direct answer. "Our intentions are absolutely friendly," they say; "We want to work with your management." If pressed, they say they've never even considered the use of force, so intent are they on a friendly deal (and confident it can be accomplished) — all very positive, but still without ruling out the possibility of a tender.

I'd advise Mr. T to demand a straight answer to his question. Here's one way to put it:

"Look, Mr. A, if you're willing to rule out force, I can let my hair down and we can have some candid discussions to see if this proposal makes any sense. But if you're not willing, then I have to approach you guardedly and with a good deal of suspicion, which isn't conducive to productive negotiations."

If Mr. A says he has no hostile intentions, Mr. T is well-advised to ask for a written agreement under which, in return for Target's agreeing to hold discussions and provide confidential information, Acquiror promises not to buy any Target shares, make any tender offer, or otherwise seek control without Target board approval, for a period of several years. (If the agreement can be so phrased as to rule out uninvited merger proposals also, Target is even better off.) If Mr. A equivocates and won't sign the agreement, then Mr. T knows he has a real problem.

BUYING TARGET'S STOCK

Should Acquiror buy some shares of Target in the market prior to the meeting? (Assume that the existence of such purchases would be disclosed at the first meeting, either voluntarily by Mr. A or in response to Mr. T's query on the subject.) Many acquisition-minded people think this is a fine way to demonstrate their seriousness of purpose. And owning the stock can be beneficial to Acquiror, either as a relatively low-cost base should a bidding contest develop, or as a means of making a profit if Target ends up in the hands of a well-heeled white knight.

But, if Acquiror isn't prepared to put Target into play, and its only hope is pulling off a friendly deal, my advice to Mr. A is not to buy Target's stock. No single act of a purchaser is viewed with more hostility by a target than the purchase of its shares. It represents a tremendous obstacle to persuading Mr. T that Acquiror's intentions are honorable.

WHAT PRICE TO PROPOSE

If Mr. A gets to the stage of actually making a proposal, a critical question for him is the matter of price. Should he, right at the outset, put his best price on the table — an offer that Mr. T "can't refuse" (although the Mr. T's of the world frequently do) — in order to exert maximum pressure on Target? If so, Acquiror will not only forego any opportunity to make the acquisition on more reasonable terms, but will have nothing left in his pocket should a real negotiation develop. On the other hand, if Mr. A chooses a more modest price — well below what he's willing to pay — he runs the risk of Mr. T proceeding on that basis, which makes it easier for Target's board to find the proposal inadequate and turn it down flat.

Here's how I like to approach this subject, when advising Acquiror. I tell my client that there are four separate numbers to determine in advance:

First, the price that Acquiror would like to pay and that it's not unreasonable to believe Target may accept (let's call this the "realistic price") — not a pipe dream, but a full, fair price, because that's what it will take to buy this company.

Second, the highest price that Acquiror would be willing to pay if it stretched to the fullest extent (the "stretched price");

Third, the price that Acquiror wants to see contained in a public announcement of the proposal (the "public price");

And fourth, Acquiror's opening offer (the "negotiating price").

I start out by asking Acquiror's executives about their realistic price. Chances are, they have one in mind. It can usually be found in the pro forma financials prepared by Acquiror's accountants. The main thing is to make sure it's in the realm of reality.

Then I ask about the stretched price. There should be some room between these two numbers, or the negotiating alternatives become very limited. But this isn't an easy figure to pry out of Acquiror (as we saw in the earlier essay, "Negotiating with Your Own Client"). The chief executive may not have faced up to the issue, in hopes that he'll never have to. Or the officers fear that the mere mention of the upper limit to their advisers will become a self-fulfilling prophecy. But, since Target is unlikely to be thrilled over the prospect of being acquired, the stretched price may be necessary to get a deal done; and knowledge of it is crucial in framing the negotiating price and any subsequent concessions — so, this issue should be resolved, at least on a preliminary basis.

Now, if and when Acquiror goes public with its proposal, I think the public price should be close to the realistic price. If the disclosed offer is too thin, it doesn't create the kind of pressure on Target's board that's needed – pressure from stockholders, arbitrageurs, and analysts urging the directors not to pass up a desirable deal. You only get one shot at this pressure, I remind the client, so don't keep more than a dollar or two in reserve for cutting a deal, should Target decide to negotiate.

The initial negotiating price ought to be close to, but not as much as, the public price. This provides slightly more room to maneuver without exceeding the realistic price, if Target negotiates; but it's not a lowball bid that's easy for Target to ignore — or to go through the motions of reviewing and rejecting, on the basis of an investment banking opinion that the offer is "grossly inadequate." If Acquiror's initial overtures are rejected by Mr. T, and Mr. A then decides to deliver a written proposal, the increase from negotiating price to public price gives Mr. T an opportunity to reverse field without losing face.

So, for example, assume that Target's per share market price is around $25. Acquiror's realistic price might be $38 per share; its stretched price, $40; its public price $36.50; and its negotiating price $35. As you can see, the range is relatively narrow. This is not the time to be chintzy. Mr. A should not deceive himself that there will be plenty of opportunity to increase his price, because there may not be. Forcing an acquisition with an unwilling suitor, without resorting to a hostile offer, is an expensive business.

RANGES AND COME-ONS

Some businessmen like to express their price thinking in terms of a range. Mr. A might say initially, for instance, that he wants to do a deal in the $32-$35 area. His rationale is that, making a subsequent $35 offer will then represent a concession on his part, since it's at the top end of the range. As a result, he has a little more room to bargain before getting into the painful numbers north of $35.

The counter-argument is that if Mr. T is an astute negotiator, he will rightly consider this proposal tantamount to an offer at the top of the range, and will give Mr. A little or no credit for the subsequent journey there. When I'm in Mr. T's shoes, I often emphasize the point by characterizing Mr. A's proposal as "your $35 offer" in the ensuing discussion, neglecting his range entirely. (For this reason, it's clearly folly for Mr. A to start with a range whose upper limit *exceeds* his selected negotiating price.) In addition, a range detracts from the cloak of definitiveness in which most purchasers like to wrap their intentions, though it may be suitable for the "aw shucks" vagueness of the afterthought approach.

Executives in Mr. A's position often worry that their initial offer will be scoffed at by Mr. T. As a result, they tend to express the number (perhaps unconsciously) in almost apologetic tones. That's the wrong approach. My advice is, once you've selected a fair negotiating price — even though you're prepared to go higher — treat it with respect. Propose it with self-confidence. Suffuse it with appropriate rationale. Mr. T is entitled to disagree with Mr. A's judgment — one expects nothing less from an astute seller — but no word, inflection or gesture of Mr. A's should suggest that this is anything other than a responsible position with which to open the bidding.

If Mr. T does disparage Mr. A's first offer at the negotiating price, Mr. A can always respond by stating he's at this level because Acquiror lacks in-depth information about Target; he's confident, however, that if Target were to furnish Acquiror with projections and other items of non-public information, supporting values in excess of what can be gleaned from the public files, then the price Acquiror is willing to pay could well be increased. This approach also finds its way into written proposals, where the public price is less than the realistic price. It's designed to suggest that more dollars may be obtained through friendly negotiations (though they probably won't be made available in the hostile takeover that Acquiror hasn't quite forsworn), and to tempt Mr. T and Target's board to reach out for them.

FINAL THOUGHTS

Where things go from here is anybody's guess — and basically beyond the scope of this article, except for two final observations.

For Mr. A, the purpose of all this maneuvering is to get a negotiation going. To succeed in that goal may require him to transgress some basic axioms of bargaining.

For example, we all know the adage that you shouldn't bid against yourself. But, let's say that Mr. T, while rejecting Mr. A's negotiating price as inadequate, implies that he may well be interested in a deal at a much higher level. Now, the classic next step by Mr. A — getting Mr. T to name his price, so as to create a bid and asked range — may be inadvisable under these circumstances. The last thing Mr. A wants is for Mr. T to dig himself into a hole (say, with a $50 price tag), from which the return to reality might cause a serious loss of face. The wiser course might be for Mr. A to give ground grudgingly on the road to his realistic price, checking all the while for signs of whether he's whetting Mr. T's interest.

For Mr. T, the optimum result is for Mr. A to go away quietly, leaving Target safe and sound until another day. If Mr. T comes to the realization that this can't be accomplished, then he faces a difficult decision — whether to be put in play, with uncertain results (including the identity of his ultimate merger partner), but at least a chance of remaining independent; or whether to negotiate the best deal possible with Acquiror, free from the spotlight glare of a public auction. Mr. T's answer often turns on such essentially subjective criteria as whether he believes Mr. A will force the issue into the public arena, and how negative Mr. T is about the prospect of eventually working for Mr. A.

*   *   *

So, strike up the band — here comes the Acquisition Two-Step of the '80s.

THE MANY FACETED
M&A LAWYER

It helps, of course, to have attended law school; but for many of the crucial roles M&A lawyers are called upon to play nowadays, some other form of higher education — usually obtained through on-the-job training — may be equally significant.

Many areas of legal practice are difficult, though I can't think of any as complex as mergers and acquisitions. But what's interesting about the M&A complexity is that much of it derives from disciplines not traditionally considered basic to a lawyer's makeup.

The strictly legal questions in M&A work, while tricky enough — and with judicial outcomes that may be far from predictable — are rarely obscure or tortuous. And, for the most part, the skills commonly associated with the legal profession — such as drafting agreements and disclosure documents, conducting due diligence reviews — play an important, but far from exceptional role.

To be fair, the litigation aspect — meat and potatoes for the bar — is absolutely central in the realm of contested takeovers. Here, lawyers do what they're trained for, with a lot riding on the outcome of crucial motions, and intense time pressure compressing what might otherwise be months of discovery, depositions, brief writing and motion practice into a couple of weeks.

Also, on the traditional front, mergers test a lawyer's negotiating skills to the utmost. Unfortunately, not all

lawyers are superior negotiators, although those who ply this particular trade should be.

Still, an abundance of non-traditional roles — ranging from public relations expert to financial whiz to psychologist — exert a continual tug on the M&A lawyer, who (at least in these areas) is often flying by the seat of his pants.

Here are ten such roles I've identified.

1. Financial Whiz. It wasn't so long ago that, when you asked a lawyer working on a public acquisition, "What does the $58.50 per share work out to, in terms of total dollars to be paid by the acquiror?", he would look back at you with a blank stare — as if to say, "Why are you bothering me with those *numbers?*" He was, after all, the *lawyer*; his area of expertise was the *legal* part of the deal; and numbers — even such crucial ones as the purchase price — were simply items that he plugged in to the proxy statement once the financial people worked them out.

(In a way, one could draw an analogy between that attitude and the disdain many lawyers used to show for *billing*. Somehow, it was beneath them professionally to have to deal with such matters of *commerce*; as a result, unbilled time would just keep accumulating — sometimes, even after the case was over. We all know how *that* has now changed!)

Well, it's a different world today in the public arena, particularly in connection with contested deals. So many of the significant conceptual points and key tactical decisions are financial or numbers-driven, to wit: comparing values between a partial and an any-and-all offer, or between one complex security and another; deciding how much the present worth of a security can be changed by tinkering with such variables as interest rate and sinking fund; determining how many shares will move from one receptacle to another at various offered prices; and even trying to figure out how a poison pill would really *work*, if tested! Questions involving figures are simply omnipresent. Lawyers who duck them — who close their eyes, claiming, "Hey, these are 'financial' matters, and I never even took accounting in law school" — are missing out on much of the tactical and negotiating action.

As a result, budding M&A lawyers with a joint J.D./M.B.A. background start with a significant advantage in their grasp of matters financial. Single sheepskin associates shouldn't be too concerned, though, since the current big-bucks mania on Wall Street seems to be luring many of these twin-degree worthies out of the law firm closet into the heady world of investment banking.

Finance is an area where the appearance of omniscience may block useful information from entering your brain. Not that I advocate gaping like a dummy in front of your client or adversary; but, in the privacy of your office or on a phone line, it's perfectly okay to seek some guidance on what's being discussed among the financial types, in order to appreciate the significance of various permutations. In other words, you're allowed to ask the investment banker, "Hey, Joe, tell me why this discounted cash flow analysis comes out so differently from using the current earnings multiple."

Your reading habits can undergo some changes also. Reading about the trials and tribulations — the triumphs and goofs — of your legal colleagues in the new-style periodicals is great sport, to be sure; but in terms of a learning experience, devouring in-depth pieces about the deals currently being done which appear in the *financial press* — exploring the rationale behind the numbers — may actually be of greater practical benefit.

2. Public Relations Expert. I came from the old school, which considered the financial press as strictly an annoyance, to be avoided if possible — but, in any case, relatively neutral in terms of substantive significance.

"You don't win this one in the newspapers," was the classic refrain. Most of the time, you ducked reporters, putting out only whatever bare minimum press releases were legally required.

There was, to be sure, a legal dimension to this approach — a good deal of concern over such potential SEC problems as gun-jumping and pre-solicitation activities (which today seem more honored in the breach). The operative by-word then was, "The less said, the better."

In recent years, however, I've learned how out-of-date that view is — especially in a contested (or potentially contested) acquisition. The reason is simple: what appears in the newspaper can have a major impact, pro or con, on what you're trying to accomplish. In today's world, individuals and institutions in a position to take actions that might affect your deal not only read the papers, but act on what they read. I don't just mean your average Joe, with a few shares at risk — I'm talking about arbitrageurs, other parties to a deal or contest, potential bidders, regulatory agencies, and even judges who end up deciding important transactional issues (boy, do I have a story to tell about *that!*). And the inescapable fact is that everyone else in the deal is getting in his licks — telling the story *his* way, with his emphasis and his nuances.

Let's face it, reporters are always looking for a hook to hang their story on; and the players who know how to feed reportorial appetites come off looking very good indeed. It's not that newsmen are biased; it's that they take their news where they find it. A reporter can't build his story around your client's declining to comment — which, in addition, often carries with it a flavor of guilty knowledge on the client's part.

I was handling a big deal not long ago for a company whose executives didn't know how to play the financial press, but were up against several masters of the craft. We were getting crucified in the papers; our side of the story wasn't getting out, and it was costing us. What the hell, I decided, we can't do worse than we're doing now. So I started to talk to reporters; and all of a sudden, a lot more balance began to appear in the news items.

I felt this was a proper role for a lawyer to be playing. I was able to decide whether it was an appropriate day to make any comment at all (on many days, official silence was still the wisest course), or whether I wanted my remarks to be strictly on background, with no attribution to the company — perhaps just "a source close to the negotiations" — or semi-anonymous (attributed to an unnamed spokesman for the company), or, if I thought something positive needed saying, coming from me directly — provided the reporter read the quote back to me for a final check. These are just the kinds of judgments that should be made by a lawyer, who is trained to refrain from saying things that can come back to bite his client in the behind.

Of course, the lawyer has to have enough of a public relations sense to know what to say (and what to avoid). A good financial public relations consultant can be helpful here, as can the investment banker.

Once the reporters knew I was willing to hear them out, they would contact me when something significant happened, or even when they had gotten some choice information from one of the other parties, thereby giving me a chance to tell our side of the story — an opportunity we might not have had if our *modus operandi* was official silence. And it's no secret that any rebuttal you make has to appear in the *same* article as the other guy's charge — tomorrow is too late, since investors have already acted upon the first story and your after-the-fact response comes across sounding weak and defensive.

Some players in the M&A game do their best negotiating in the press — sending all kinds of signals, justifying their positions, and so on. When you see something in the paper like, "Sources indicate that Consolidated will have to raise its price to win the Silicon deal, or it risks getting a reputation for blowing the big ones," or "Conglomerate is reported to have offered Target an additional $3 per share if Target would go quietly," rest assured, these musings didn't just pop out of thin air — somebody is out there doing his thing, and you're well-advised to level the playing field.

3. Writer. In a similar vein, today's M&A lawyers need to be able to string words together with some real sensitivity to the nuances. Attorneys accustomed to writing dry-as-dust prospectuses or drafting clear-but-cold agreements may not necessarily be skilled in manipulating the English language around tricky corners and into meaningful nooks and crannies.

Moreover, bare bones press releases can easily be misconstrued by reporters and readers. Nor can you rely on things being fleshed out in subsequent interviews between reporter and executive — they may miss connections, and anyway, you can never be sure what the executive will say.

So, if you've got something to put out — such as justifying, through a logical explanation, why your client took the action he did — then take the time to write it out yourself. Don't worry that the press release may run to some length; I did one that came to 11 pages, but as a result, the papers played the story just the way I wanted them to.

It's not only writings intended for the press that call on these particular skills. Other documents, of less defined stripe than an agreement, require a subtle touch. Take the so-called "bear-hug" letter, by which an aggressor attempts simultaneously to court a prospective target and to threaten putting the company into play. [See the prior essay, "The Acquisition Mating Dance."] What message do you want to get across? How close can you come to committing your client, without actually doing so? What do you say in order to make the other side worried about having to make a public disclosure, while still giving their lawyer enough ammunition to advise his client that they don't have to speak out should negotiations get started? And so on.

You don't need to be Herman Melville — and I'm not suggesting that "creative" writing is the order of the day — but a little attention to prose style is definitely called for.

4. Psychologist. To the financial world, they may appear to be companies; but in the trenches, many of these entities are little more than the extended personality of one or two individuals. And the ability to predict how these protagonists will react to certain stimuli, or to foresee their next move, or to figure out how to persuade them to move in your direction — or even just to devise a means of getting someone to meet with your client — is a constant preoccupation at the higher levels of deal-making.

Here's an area where we're all amateurs, and yet it's extremely rare to get help from a psychiatrist or other professional trained in psychological counseling — even though their use has become relatively common in such areas as jury selection.

So, it often falls to the lawyer — who is expected to be good at such things, perhaps because of his experience at the negotiating table — to peer deeply into the mind of the key person on the other side. The problem is, though, that you may *not* be sitting across the table from your adversary — a much broader gulf (both in spatial and motivational terms) often separates the combatants. And the useful psychological insights you have picked up through bargaining over the years — strictly on a seat-of-the-pants basis — may be less useful in the context of utilizing force to achieve or resist unshared goals.

By the way, it's not just understanding the motivations and hot buttons of the guy on the *other* side of the deal; it's those of your own client, too. Lawyers who operate on the premise that abstract rationality dictates all reactions and movements in the emotion-laden world of corporate takeovers do so at their peril.

5. Moralist. A traditional role for the lawyer is keeper of the corporate conscience — deciding what behavior will pass muster and what flips over the line. In the old days, however, this task was much more straightforward than at present. The conflict of interest issues today are very subtle and slippery, often lacking ready precedents. So, we find ourselves playing the role of moralist — imposing on the client the lawyer's own notion of what's good and bad — what passes and what flunks our individual smell test.

Here's the conflict between the controlling shareholder's stock interest and his board seat; there's the conflict between the CEO's continued employment and his role as chairman of the board; and everywhere are the myriad conflicts arising in the context of an LBO — it's not always clear who's buying and who's selling! — which are particularly tough for the lawyer in the middle.

These conflicts play right into such tough questions as, "Do we sell the Company or try to stay independent?" or "Can we negotiate the CEO's employment contract before we've reached a deal on the merger?" or "Should management come in with its best bid on the LBO the first time around?" — all of which ultimately end up demanding Solomon-like judgment from — who else? — the lawyer.

Ethics we can handle, but morality — that may be another matter.

6. Employee Benefits Consultant. Along the same lines, some of the most perplexing issues faced by counsel in an acquisition involve the personal benefits to be received by members of the acquired company's management. And it's not so much a matter of negotiating those benefits with the *acquiring* corporation; rather, it's a question of the employment contract or severance arrangement that the executive works out in advance with his *own* company — usually with the blessing of the compensation committee of the board of directors.

But before anything goes to the committee, it's up to management to formulate the specific terms — and that's where the lawyer comes in. What's appropriate under the circumstances? Should the executive get three years' salary in the event he's canned, or only two? Should the benefits include a tax gross-up if the numbers exceed the IRS guidelines and trigger the prohibitive tax?

These would be tough questions for expert employee benefit consultants; they're even tougher for a non-expert lawyer caught in the middle between an executive who's anxious about job security and fair treatment, and the board (the lawyer's ultimate client) which will undoubtedly ask counsel his opinion of the terms and whether they'll stand up if challenged in the courts.

It's no good to punt — you have to speak out on these issues. And the really tough part comes when you think management has gotten a little too greedy — which is definitely *not* what they want to hear coming from their lawyer.

7. Stock Market Analyst. So many of the moves made in a public acquisition are geared to their effect on the stock market. "If we bid $50, will the arbs go for it?" "How much higher do we have to go to get the stock flowing in?" "How many shares can we pick up if we do a Street sweep?"

Now, what's likely to happen in the market is the particular bailiwick of investment banking firms, but it's by no means an exact science; and sometimes your guess is as good as the next banker's. Moreover, you need to appreciate how the market works, or you'll find yourself proffering a suggestion that others hoot down on the grounds that it won't fly with the market professionals.

My word of advice here is, don't formulate plans that only work if the market behaves in a predictable manner — you'll be doomed to disappointment. Instead, stay flexible, ready to jump in a different direction and pull your irons out of the fire if — as so often is the case — the market action simply defies rational analysis.

8. Businessman.   Just as the line between law and finance has become blurred, so the distinction between legal and business issues is no longer clear-cut.

For example, many acquisitions today depend on the acquiror's ability to sell off big chunks of the target's assets in order to pay down the debt incurred to make the acquisition. The lawyer needs to get actively involved in this business planning, in order to be able to assess the likelihood of his client accomplishing this task — to say nothing of passing on the adequacy of the applicable disclosures in the tender offer papers or proxy statements.

Similarly, lawyers representing targets and white knights have to deal with the question of whether some key segment of the seller's business can be separately encapsulated, to serve as the basis for a "crown jewel" option intended to lock up the deal as against the hostile bidder and all other contenders. Crown jewels — which are usually negotiated in the heat of battle, under great pressure to come to a rapid determination — have become a hot target for litigious disgruntled suitors, who attack the price, directorial due care, and the bid-chilling aspects of the option. Real business problems abound here, involving valuation, the severability of the unit, the ability of the target to function without it, and so on. The lawyers must appreciate the business realities involved in order to structure the transaction to withstand legal attack.

9. Generalissimo.   In the context of contested take-overs, the analogies between running a deal and conducting a military campaign are often frightening. The lingo is that of war; the attitudes of the combatants may well be similar to hostile belligerents; and the strategic and tactical thinking is much more von Clausewitz than Albert Schweitzer.

To be sure, other traditional lawyers' functions sometimes approximate aspects of warfare. Any litigation involves combat; still, its typical concern with past events, its non-monopolization of management attention, and its lack of certain more subtle dimensions analogize more to a single battle than an extended campaign. Negotiations may approximate the diplomacy that often accompanies warfare, but lack the mood of imminent peril should the talks fail, as well as the sense of total mobilization.

With a takeover, however, you get the feeling you're in the middle of World War II. There are allies and foes, pitched battles and periods of anticipation, intelligence operations, problems with lines of supply, diplomatic initiatives, moves taken to win over the "hearts and minds," threats, bluffs, and so on.

For those of us who were too young for World War II, in college during Korea, and too old for Viet Nam — and for everyone else with unsated bellicose impulses — this takeover stuff is hard to put down — especially since there are no draftees, and regardless of the outcome (in contrast to the real thing), you come back in one piece and well-compensated for your time and trouble.

10. Seer. It used to be that the rules of the game were clearly marked out, and your job was to lead the client by the hand in complying. But now, it's not always clear what rules we're playing by.

This became most apparent in 1986 in the realm of taxes. Everyone knew there were changes in the wind that could greatly alter the shape of things, but no one was sure what would emerge from Congress — both on a substantive level, and also in terms of retroactivity.

So, we were all playing the role of seer then, trying to peer into the future and figure out what was going to happen. And the stakes were high. If the desired tax treatment wasn't going to be available — for instance, in the case of a company selling its assets in the course of what was formerly a Section 337 liquidation — the net difference could run into many millions of dollars.

If we *knew* the old treatment wasn't going to be available, then perhaps we could have designed around it (at some financial loss, or decrease of flexibility, to be sure) or conducted negotiations to spread the damage around, so to speak. But we didn't know that, which left us in a terrible pickle.

All we could do was gather the best information available on the mood of the Congress; explain the situation to our client; have him say, "What do you think we ought to do?"; take a stab at a solution; gulp as we saw it implemented; and hold our breath, hoping the bill came out the right way.

This all goes to the issue of the lawyer's predictive function — traditionally, one of his strong points. Being able to tell a client how something is likely to come out separates the professional from the layman; and while it's by no means the whole of lawyering, it furnishes a sturdy foundation on which to base considerations of strategy and approach. In today's fast-paced world, that foundation is eroding.

I might add that the lawyer's predictive function vis-a-vis takeover litigation — again, one of his classic strong points — is also a bit shaky now, in view of some surprising decisions and judicial language that isn't always crystal clear. Put a bunch of lawyers together in a room, and try to get them to agree on just how the Delaware court is likely to come out on the *next* set of facts it's faced with — you'll see exactly what I mean.

*   *   *

So, there it is — a quiver of skills that no one ever told you, back then, you would need, but which in large part serves to make M&A practice something special.

WHO WANTS THE DEAL MORE?

My wife, Barbara Fox, who runs a residential real estate company and is one of New York's top brokers, happens to be a terrific negotiator. She has that rare ability to go right to the brink ("Listen, Mr. Jones, if this is your final position, it's a shame, but that's life; Mrs. Smith wishes you good luck — you'll need it!. . ."), with such seeming insouciance, that the other party really *believes* she'll walk away from the deal — when, in fact, she hasn't the slightest intention of doing so.

TAKING A DIVE

Two years ago, we decided to rent a house in the country to use for weekends. A local real estate broker was showing us around. I intended to leave the bargaining to Barbara, since this was right up her line.

The very first house we saw was a real winner. I could tell Barbara thought it was wonderful — just what she'd been looking for. The broker had told us what rent was being sought by the lessor — a number which seemed somewhat padded, though not unreasonable.

Since the lessor was present, I tried not to look too excited about the place, adopting a somewhat noncommittal demeanor — a counterbalance to Barbara, who was doing a lot of uncharacteristic gushing, considering the pending negotiation.

116

My bright-as-a-button ten-year-old niece happened to be along. I whispered some instructions to her; she nodded wisely. A few minutes later, when both the lessor and broker were within earshot, I asked her: "Alexis, what do you think of this place?" "It's pretty nice," she replied, "but" — and here her cadence slowed as she enunciated each word, "IT'S AWFULLY CLOSE TO THE ROAD."

Good girl, I thought; we're going to set things up real nice. "Is this the *only* closet in the bedroom?" I inquired, dismay tinging my voice. You could almost feel the tension building, as I prepared to wax eloquent on the inadequacies of the refrigerator.

"We'll take it!" Barbara suddenly announced with a flourish. "Where do we sign?"

In the inevitable post mortem, I raised the question (in the most gentle, understanding, husbandly fashion, of course) as to why Barbara — negotiator *par excellence* — had taken such a complete and rapid dive. Her reply was disarmingly candid: "I really wanted that house."

Well, it's the old story. Surgeons shouldn't operate on their kids; a lawyer who represents himself has a fool for a client; and negotiators with personal interests at stake are hard put to generate the detachment needed to persuade their adversary of the necessity for concessions.

Viewing this issue from the perspective of a lawyer who acts as negotiator for a client, a crucial question to ask yourself — in planning strategy, giving advice, taking positions, and evaluating developments — is, who wants this deal more? Is it your client or the guy on the other side? And how strongly does each of them feel about it?

Unfortunately, this is the kind of motivational question that many lawyers, who are otherwise skilled in the technical aspects of their craft, fail to address. And the answer may not always be as readily apparent as it was with our country house, since a lot of acting and posturing — even self-deception — goes on at the client level.

THREE DIFFERENT SITUATIONS

Let's examine this in the context of a business negotiation between a seller and a prospective buyer, relating to the sale of a company, or a parcel of real estate, or any one-of-a-kind asset. In order to appreciate certain dynamics of this kind of negotiation — which is the kind that lawyers get involved in — it's helpful first to contrast it with two other common sales situations.

The most rigid set-up occurs in the seller's regular course of business operations, involving a product (like a major appliance) that isn't unique (in that the seller has multiple units and competitive products are sold elsewhere). Here, the pressure is on the seller, who definitely needs to sell — that's the reason he's in business. He may start from a list price, but unless it violates store policy or there's a shortage or monopoly situation, he'll probably have to give this buyer a discount if he wants to make the sale. The buyer's in the driver's seat here.

The second situation involves a vendor selling a relatively unique item (such as an oil painting or a piece of antique jewelry) as part of the regular course of his business. The seller's still in the business of selling, and can't even take solace in a clearly definable list price; the buyer *knows* he'll be able to negotiate. (In fact, the seller probably has to load the initial price so that when he backs off, the buyer will think he's getting a bargain.) But the buyer who yearns for this item is actually less in command here. He can't find the same item elsewhere; and he has to worry that it may not be here too long either. The seller has a hook into him, which savvy vendors use shamelessly. ("Better make up your mind now, because I've got another customer coming in later today who's very interested in the same item. . .")

Now, the situation in which lawyers play a role usually involves a unique item, such as a business or property, being sold by a seller who's *not* in the business of selling such items. The working assumption is that he doesn't have to sell the property — he may not even have considered it until approached by the buyer — and if the deal being negotiated doesn't go through, he may revert to just being an owner. Moreover, unlike the first two situations — in which the buyer knows there's a deal if he's willing to pay the vendor's price — this seller hasn't agreed (even implicitly, at least until he discloses what he's willing to accept) to take any particular price.

So, the buyer is at more of a disadvantage here than in the first two situations. Assuming the buyer really likes the property, and the seller plays his cards right, the buyer may have to stretch a lot on price to make the deal. (That's the bad news for the buyer; the good news — admittedly, falling more into the psychological than the financial realm — is that such stretching is easier for him to justify in this isolated-sale context, since it's often difficult to assess what is fair and what's overpriced.) Also, unlike the first two situations in which the seller's warranties are provided as a matter of course, the buyer here has to bargain for any protection he gets — which often makes for as tough an additional negotiation as that previously occurring over price.

THE BUYER . . . OR THE SELLER?

Now, returning to our topic, one of the real keys to how the bargaining comes out in this situation is which party wants the deal more. And, in many cases, it's the *buyer.* Consider, for example, this typical scenario.

The seller is about to part with "his baby" — the business that he built up from nothing over 30 years. He's bound to have mixed emotions about selling. And we've all seen how someone who really doesn't want to do something — whether his feelings have already surfaced or are still unconscious — can come up with lots of reasons justifying inaction.

For example, this seller may become mesmerized by his own swollen asking price, and then use the buyer's unwillingness to pay it as the excuse to break off negotiations — reckoning that he'll get top dollar from another buyer, or convincing himself he's unwilling to sell at a lesser price. Or he may dig in his heels (and even end the talks) if he perceives the buyer — or the buyer's lawyer! — as negotiating too hard for the kind of protection that buyers commonly think they need.

Meanwhile, examine the buyer in the same scenario. While the seller ends up with just money or paper (pretty prosaic stuff), the buyer is out there trying to acquire a dream, to breathe life into a fantasy — buying a company that's a perfect fit with his other businesses, or that gives him a toehold in a long-sought marketplace. And there's a ready rationalization for such a buyer in shelling out more dollars; he's paying so much already, what's a few extra bucks? — particularly when (unlike a refrigerator) there's no price tag hanging from the item being purchased. Or, why not give in on some of those protections he's been seeking? That's all lawyer stuff anyway, and none of those eventualities is likely to come to pass. . . .

Now, on the other hand, there may be instances when it's the *seller* who wants the deal more. Perhaps he really needs the money, prosaic though cash may be. Or, he sees black clouds on the horizon (the Japanese have duplicated his technology) and wants to get out before the deluge. Or, he realizes that this buyer is nibbling at a top-dollar price, and he doesn't want to let him off the hook —

particularly since there may not be other bidders for a basically unique business that's unlikely to fit into many buyers' plans.

The *buyer*, in this second scenario, may be a little more cautious. After all, the price seems quite high, the horizon is murky, the seller appears anxious. . . .

WHO MOVES . . . AND WHO STANDS FIRM?

The determination of who wants it more is most relevant to the bargaining over price. To state the obvious, the seller generally wishes to receive more than the buyer would like to pay; the buyer wants to pay less than the seller would like to receive. They start off some distance apart; to make a deal, there has to be movement toward the middle. Usually, both parties move at least some of the way, since no one wants to do a deal in which he's been unable to bargain for *anything* off (or over) his adversary's initial proposal. The real question is, who will move *more*? And conversely, who will — at a point when he seems to have too little (or too much) on the table to make the deal — stand firm?

So, for instance, assume you're advising the seller. There have been several rounds of movement toward the center; the last was made by the buyer. Now, it's the seller's turn. You assess the situation. Your client doesn't have to do the deal. His inital asking price wasn't outrageous, and he's made some meaningful concessions as the bargaining has progressed. The buyer, on the other hand, gives every sign of badly wanting the deal — and doesn't appear tapped out in terms of funds.

Well, this might be an ideal point to advise the seller to pause, stand firm, and see if he can get the buyer to bid against himself.

The same process applies in terms of other negotiable items, once the price is resolved. Let's say you represent the buyer this time. A battle is raging over a certain protection your client would like to have — though you reckon that, in the final analysis, he could do without it.

You size things up. The seller has achieved a nifty price that he's unlikely to duplicate elsewhere. You have a hunch he's under some financial pressure. The issue being debated involves a contingency that may or may not happen; the buyer's position isn't unreasonable. And — of prime importance — you feel that, despite the emotion he's displaying over this issue, the seller is basically a rational individual, who's likely to behave in accordance with his economic best interests.

Well, it's not a bad place for the buyer to draw the line. People rarely give up a deal over non-price issues, unless the other party's position is totally egregious, or unless they don't care that much about the deal in the first place. This seller cares; the buyer's position isn't that extreme; the seller can't take a chance that you just might mean business. The buyer can stick, with reasonable confidence that the seller will come around.

CANDOR WITH THE CLIENT

Sometimes, though, the assessment goes the other way; and you, as the objective counselor, face the difficult task of advising your client that *he's* the party who wants or needs the deal more — and consequently, that he ought to go up (or down) on price, or collapse on some other hotly contested issue. Of course, you can't really tell your client how badly he wants something. What you can do is help him arrive at that realization on his own, by putting the particular issue — be it price or whatever — in context. ("I know it's painful, Paul, but think of it this way: The increment they're demanding is less than two percent of what you're already prepared to pay. If the decision to buy is a good one at $10 million, does another $180,000 make it wrong?")

You can also help your client size up the guy on the other side. Presumably, you've been listening to what's been said, peering behind the words, assessing the actions (more important than the words), piecing together the clues. What's the net? ("Bottom line, Paul, it's my feeling that the seller is very ambivalent on doing this deal; in fact, he may be looking for an excuse to call it off. The $180,000 may furnish him with just that excuse. . . .")

So, that's the way it goes. And you want to know something? My wife, Barbara — whom I still enjoy chiding over her capitulation — was right! We enjoyed that house thoroughly. If we had hung tough and the lessor had nowhere else to go, we might have knocked $50-$100 per month off the rent — but, by the same token, we might also have lost the place to another couple who loved the place and were willing to pay the tab.

And by the way — as Alexis will confess, if pushed — it really wasn't *that* close to the road. . . .

BRIDGING TROUBLED WATERS

I spend most of my professional hours negotiating mergers and other business deals. Lately, though I've gotten involved in trying to resolve some commercial disputes, both before and after litigation has begun.

Going in, I thought this wouldn't be too difficult. Cutting up a finite pie seemed a lot easier than pulling together all the pieces of a complicated transaction. But I was dead wrong. Resolving disputes is damn hard work — in some respects even harder than making a deal. Still, I found that my experience in putting deals together did give me a fresh perspective on the settlement process.

PROBLEMS IN RESOLVING DISPUTES

The difficulties in resolving conflicts amicably, without resort to a judge, jury or arbitrator, fall into two broad categories: those that are inherent in the contested situation itself; and those related to the problem of finding an acceptable compromise.

INHERENT IN THE SITUATION

The inherent difficulties include the client's attitude of ambivalence, the special problems a litigator faces, the

126

tricky matter of getting talks going, the mood of distrust, and the absence of a "can do" mentality.

Ambivalence. What struck me first was how ambivalent people were — right up to the moment of final settlement — as to whether or not the matter should be settled.

In a business deal such as an acquisition, the prevailing mood is, "let's get it done." All the pressure drives the parties to arrive at an agreement, to consummate the closing. The businessmen want the deal done yesterday; the investment bankers sweat over their contingent fees; and the lawyers get caught up in the frenzy. The emphasis is on being "constructive" — finding ways to resolve the impasse and get on with the transaction. A lawyer whose heart isn't in it — who tries to delay (or worse, sabotage) agreement — is anathema. The *bete noir* of all concerned is a "busted deal."

Where the parties are at loggerheads in a dispute, however, the mood is entirely different. I sense it's not untypical for at least one of the parties (or his lawyer) to prefer that the conflict remain unresolved — and he invariably turns out to be the guy on the *other* side! Perhaps he has something to gain in another sphere from continuance of the litigation, such as imposing pressure on a business competitor.

But even the party who has *more* to gain from a negotiated settlement often appears ambivalent about settling. One minute, he tells you to go ahead and see what you can work out; the next, he has second thoughts and is ready to go back to war.

Settling differences is tough enough if your heart's really in it. When lawyers reflect their clients' hot-and-cold moods, the task becomes monumental.

Litigators' Problems. If you think about it, the real keys for a lawyer in settling a dispute are, first, to overcome his own client's ambivalence and get him committed to a settlement, and second, to come up with a proposed resolution that satisfies his adversary sufficiently to give up the fight.

The litigator who is handling the case (assuming it has ripened into a lawsuit) bears a special burden in accomplishing these tasks. Up to now, he has been busy throwing his weight around: alleging total fraud and depredation, seeking trebled recompense, ridiculing his adversary's claims as lacking merit. The litigation papers — with everything larger than life and choking on adverbs (the opponent's argument is "patently absurd," the simplest contractual phrase is "hopelessly ambiguous") — are enough to send shivers up a corporate lawyer's spine. And the litigators, who tend to be combative types, manifest the indignation of their respective clients — so that most contacts during the lawsuit have probably been of the bristling variety.

To shift abruptly from all this to talking about settlement requires a sizable psychological adjustment. What makes it even more difficult is that the lawyers have no way of knowing whether a settlement will ultimately be reached. The left hand is negotiating while the right prepares to resume the conflict. I think this uncertainty deters trial lawyers from taking positions that imply vulnerability, from swapping meaningful concessions — even from making conciliatory noises — for fear that such gestures will somehow make things more difficult if they have to go back to the mat.

In short, there can be a rigidity in shepherding the litigation that is antithetical to the search for compromise — a search that lies at the core of striking a deal.

The litigator may also have trouble, of a more subtle variety, in his own camp. Clients like their gladiators to be tough, to stand up for them forcefully; and successful litigators often cultivate a hawkish image. Now, sure, if his client tells him to settle, a litigator can follow instructions as well as the next lawyer; but my sense is that it's very difficult for a litigator to prod his client in that direction (assuming the litigator feels that's the appropriate course). Yet, I find that many business deals get done only when the lawyers are able to move their clients away from intractable positions toward compromise solutions, in which they're giving up something to gain something else.

For a litigator — poised to defend his client's honor to the last ditch — that's a tough posture to take without running the risk of being deemed a "softy," who's afraid to litigate and is ready to give away the store.

Initiating Talks. Once litigation has commenced, I get the feeling there's often a lot of foot-shuffling prior to the initiation of settlement talks — the principal concern being that to make the first move is a display of weakness. So, each side waits for the other side to blink first, which might happen one day — and, if we wait long enough, pigs will probably fly, too.

Distrust. A crucial factor usually present in a messy dispute, which hinders the ability of lawyers to negotiate, is the distrust that each side feels for the other. I wasn't prepared for the depth of feeling on this score. Yet, in retrospect, it's perfectly natural; how else could the parties have reached this hostile impasse? The plaintiff feels terribly aggrieved by the defendant who (in the plaintiff's view) has committed a serious tort or breach of contract; the defendant, certain he has done nothing wrong, harbors a sense of betrayal at being hauled into court. What basis is there for trust between the parties?

Yet trust is basic to successful negotiating. Has each party received accurate information from the other about the subject matter of the dispute? Will a party use what he learns in the negotiations to his adversary's disadvantage? Will the other side renege tomorrow on what he agreed to today? If the settlement involves future conduct — as it often must to bring the full range of settlement options into play — can the other party be trusted to live up to his end of the bargain? Without trust, it's tough to make a deal.

In corporate transactions, lawyers and businessmen start by assuming that they can trust their opposite numbers. In litigation, trust is hard to win and harder to maintain. But when the opposing lawyers can create an atmosphere of mutual trust, this climate can go a long way (assuming the lawyers have some influence with their clients) toward closing the gap between positions that had seemed irreconcilable. Again, I would bet this is more difficult with two litigators who have been at each other's throats right up to the point that the discussion shifts to settlement.

Sense of Solubility.   In deal-making, most good lawyers start with the attitude that everything is ultimately soluble. Sure, you have to reduce what sound like sacred princples to mundane dollars, then throw in a face-saver or two — but eventually, you expect to get all the way home. Part of this attitude is the realization that the other guy's problems are *your* problems, too. If your adversary can't solve a particular tax issue, for instance, there may be no deal at all. So you have to help the other side develop a structure that works *for him.*

This attitude of ultimate solubility is conspicuously absent in litigation. The parties' positions always seem irreconcilable — just read the briefs! There is no disposition to solve the other side's problems; everyone is having a hard enough job solving his own.

Still, the crux of accommodation is often to figure out what your adversary's *real* problem is (since he may have been less than forthcoming on this score) and then to come up with a creative solution. But my sense is that litigators, influenced by their clients' huffing and puffing, often neglect this particular thought process.

Finding an Acceptable Compromise

Now, let's turn to the other category of problems — those related to finding an acceptable compromise. This group includes difficulties in assessing the judicial alternative to resolution of the dispute, the absence of usable settlement models, and the necessarily global nature of the solution.

The Judicial Alternative. In deal-making, if negotiations prove unsuccessful, one party or the other can just walk away. This threat keeps a negotiator from taking too unreasonable a position, unless his leverage is terrific (as when the other party needs the deal to avoid being taken over by a raider).

So, when a corporate lawyer decides whether to stick or yield on certain major points, the key question is whether the issue is a "deal-breaker." If it is, then the alternative to compromise is clear: no deal. Someone has to budge if the project is worth doing; otherwise, both sides go home.

But in litigation there is no neutral walkaway. The alternative to settling is to try the case — to let the judge (or jury or arbitrator) decide. The consequences of not settling will be determined by a third party. And, at the moment you attempt to settle, no one knows for certain how the trier of fact would come out. Yet, in order to evaluate the proposed settlement, you need to assess how much your client will win or lose if you take the case to judgment.

To estimate a range of potential settlements, you not only have to evaluate how well *you* will do in the case, but also how well your adversary believes *he* will make out (which may be different from what he *says* during the negotiations.) Of course, what's in your adversary's mind can be influenced by what you do and say as you go about the process of trying to lower his expectations.

The central problem in valuing the litigation alternative is that a judge cannot just whack up the pile of dollars at issue somewhere in the middle, which is where the parties are heading when they try to settle. If the judge finds for the plaintiff, he will probably award him much of what he reasonably claims; if he finds for the defendant, the plaintiff gets nothing. So the negotiated settlement is almost bound to be at odds with the litigation result.

Thus, even if the two sides could agree on the *likely* outcome, it would not be usable as a settlement figure. The potential loser would say, "I'd rather take my chances; I sure can't do worse."

So the parties need to decide two things — the likely outcome, and just how likely it is to occur — in order to discount back to a fair settlement. These are truly tough calls, and if a jury is involved, the prospects are even more inscrutable; it's definitely not the hothouse in which negotiated solutions bloom.

Well, say some litigators, it's not all that difficult; just try the winners, and settle the losers! This reminds me of Will Rogers's advice on the stock market: "Don't gamble; take all your savings and buy some good stock and hold it till it goes up, then sell it. If it don't go up, don't buy it."

No Models. Another problem in settling litigation, as compared with negotiating a deal, is the scarcity of good models on which to rely. In an acquisition, opposing counsel argue over a number of points, but we have a plethora of precedents for how most issues are usually resolved, and these precedents provide sort of a built-in standard of reasonableness. I know what can be yielded — others have done so before me, so my client won't feel too exposed — and, conversely, where I should stand firm.

In contrast, many commercial litigation situations have their own unique facts and dynamics. While analogies may be available and damages measurable within a range, litigators often lack useful benchmarks.

The Global Solution. One reason I underestimated the difficulty of dispute resolution is that, in contrast to deal-making where it's necessary to agree on a large number of points, resolving a dispute often requires agreement on only a single dollar figure. Once the bucks are right, everything else falls into place.

I assumed that fighting over one issue would be easier than trying to sort out dozens of issues. I discovered, though, that the very narrowness of the negotiations works to your *disadvantage* in trying to resolve matters between the parties.

When the agreement depends on a single number, nothing is settled until everything is settled. In a deal, there may be a hundred issues, but they are sprinkled throughout the process; and you can make progress on them as you go — swapping A for B (or perhaps conceding A, in hopes of getting a reciprocal concession on B down the road). No single issue — other than price, which is usually the first big issue resolved — takes on disproportionate importance. In litigation, however, much more pressure is placed on the final breakthrough.

SOME THOUGHTS ON
NEGOTIATING SETTLEMENTS

Well, those are some of the problems. Here are some thoughts I had on overcoming these obstacles and resolving disputes.

The Possibility of Two Lawyers

Some of the problems referred to above *I* didn't face — coming into the litigation as a non-litigator. There was no backlog of personal hostility to overcome; I was better able to deal with the issue of distrust; and as for initiating settlement talks — why, that was just what I was there for in the first place. I simply called up the other lawyer and said, in effect, hey, let's see if it's possible to work out a negotiated settlement before my partner tears you apart in court.

In terms of dealing with the other side, I was able to come up with suggestions and fresh approaches to resolving the impasse, without carrying any special baggage from the litigation. I wasn't ambivalent at all — everyone realized my function was to try to negotiate a settlement — and I could be constructive and inclined to the everything-is-soluble approach without worrying too much about what my attitude might convey to my opposite number. Whenever I found myself too far out on a limb, I could always point to my litigating partner — the image of him I tried to convey to the other side was of a large lion just prior to feeding time — waiting impatiently in the wings for the negotiations to break down, so he could get back to the real task of stomping on our adversary in court.

As for dealing with my own client, I was able to say: Look, if you want litigation advice, my partner will tell you about the risks and rewards. If you want to know what I think it will take to settle this case, I'll tell you that. Then you can make up your mind which way you want to go.

My experience suggested to me that, at least in some cases, a two-lawyer team — a litigator and a negotiator — has a flexibility of approach that either lawyer alone lacks.

In suggesting this, I intend no disrespect to my litigating colleagues, for whom I have the utmost admiration. In particular, I find no substance in the charge sometimes leveled that litigators do not want to settle because, with all the bravado of their papers, they have talked themselves into thinking that their side of the case is stronger than it really is. In my experience, good litigators — no matter how much they may want to try the case — provide the client with a fair assessment of risks and rewards and do recommend settlement if they think that is the appropriate course. Behind all the noise and posturing, they understand what a crapshoot litigation is.

My point, though, is that it's often hard for one person to play two contrasting roles. Having a litigator-negotiator team may increase your effectiveness by allowing each person to play a single role to the hilt. This approach may also keep the other side off balance, not knowing who will prevail in the councils of your client. The team approach can also help your client to decide whether to fight or settle, since each lawyer advises him on only one of the options.

This approach calls for good teamwork. You and your partner need to be on the same wavelength, with neither of you committed to litigating or settling at any cost but realizing that the scales can tilt either way as the negotiations proceed — and understanding that ultimately, when he has all the useful inputs each of you has developed, it's the client's call which way to go.

To my mind, it's a mistake to refrain from initiating talks indefinitely out of a fear that the overture will convey weakness. Obviously, timing can be important. The day after your side has been trounced on a motion or has suffered a setback in discovery is not the best time to hoist the white flag. But, generally speaking, if it is in your client's best interests to settle, and the other side makes no move in that direction, you should try to open a dialogue.

A good litigator knows how to get across a sense of confidence in his case, so he is not unduly concerned that his adversary will perceive him as having cold feet. In fact, some litigators go one step further and suggest that they are initiating talks because they know their adversary *cannot* make the first overture — given his lousy case, it would obviously be a terrible sign of weakness for *him* to do so.

The realistic approach is to highlight the cost to both sides if the case continues and say, "Before our clients make us rich, shouldn't we look at the alternatives?" Weakness and strength will be apparent from the course of the settlement discusssions, not from who makes the first move.

Early or Late.   Is it better to try to settle the dispute before or after the lawsuit has started? There are pros and cons to both.

Settling early makes sense for a number of reasons. Starting the talks is easier before litigation begins, simply because no one *wants* to litigate if he doesn't have to. Once the lawsuit commences, picking the right time to talk can be a delicate operation. Also, at the early stage, neither party has made a big litigation investment of time, effort, or fees; the momentum and passions of the contest are yet to come, and less animosity stands in the way.

Sometimes, though, only a lawsuit can induce a recalcitrant adversary to come to the table. (But it can also work the other way. Sometimes the threat has force; but once the lawsuit has been filed, the pressure to settle dissipates, and the parties dig in for a pitched battle.)

Discovery may give you a keener sense of the strengths and weaknesses of both cases. This perspective can help you assess the case if it goes to trial. Litigation may also work off some of the parties' venom. As they see their legal bills mounting with no trial in sight, they may be more receptive to working things out.

All things being equal, I think you're better off trying to settle the dispute early, provided you can put yourself in a position to understand the relative merits of each party's case.

Preparation; Assessing the Case

It's important to prepare for negotiating a settlement. I have a feeling that many litigators, who spend countless hours preparing for trial, motions, and even depositions, spend very little time getting ready for settlement discussions. Think about it: if you're not prepared, and your adversary is, he has an advantage.

The core of good preparation for settlement is to flush out the strengths and weaknesses of both sides' cases. How do you do this without starting a lawsuit and going through discovery?

In one of the matters I handled, where the dispute was heavily fact-laden, I got each party to spell out its factual case. To be sure, there was a lot of posturing, some real vagueness in crucial spots, and (as might be expected) an absence of common ground on even the most trivial elements. Still, the exercise served an important educational function, not the least of which was to isolate the major issues, leaving us all better off than if we had been flying totally blind. It also showed everyone that the two sides could talk rationally without going to court.

Negotiating Pointers

Here are some thoughts on conducting the negotiations:

First, be persistent. There's no quick fix in settlement discussions. One case I handled involved settlement talks, interspersed by litigation maneuvers, that went on for several years. You simply have to stick with it, no matter what the frustrations. Instant gratification is for bowlers.

Second, listen. Once you get into the talks, don't do all the talking. Listen to what your adversary has to say. And particularly listen, with an analytical ear, to the unspoken messages — such as what has been curiously *omitted* from your adversary's position. You can learn a lot by creative listening.

Third, ask questions. Prepare and ask probing questions. You might get some interesting answers. At worst, your adversary's ducking and weaving, or outright refusal to answer, can itself provide useful information.

Next, equalize the authority. Make sure the other lawyer has as much authority as you do to reach a settlement — or at least has as much clout with his client as you have with yours. "I'll sell this one to my client if you sell it to yours" is a familiar refrain in negotiations. If your adversary is handicapped in this regard, watch out: the game is being played with a loaded deck.

Make an effort to persuade the other side that it's in his interest to settle. It must be in *your* interest, or you wouldn't be at the table; but your adversary may not yet be convinced that settlement is advantageous for him, too. Probe to find out why he is reluctant; then deal directly with his rationale.

Be creative. There may be things other than whacking up a pot of cash that can bring the parties together. Never underestimate the power of tax advantages. If you are unskilled in that department, bring in an expert.

Business arrangements may offer a way out. If the parties can have commercial relations, the value to the recipient of goods and services is always substantially higher than the cost to the furnisher, an economic fact of life that can help to bridge large gaps.

The subject matter of the dispute can itself provide grist for the settlement mill. If, for example, there's a question about the value of disputed property, it may be possible (if the property is divisible, such as a natural resource) to use some of it directly in the settlement, instead of reaching an impasse trying to agree on the equivalent dollar value.

Time is also significant. Payments spread out over a number of years have both a financial and psychological dimension. The recipient can say, "I settled for $5 million." The payor can say, "It cost me $3.5 million — the net present value of the payments — to get rid of the case."

If your initial discussions have isolated several difficult issues, try to attack these separately. By chopping the overall settlement into parts, you may achieve a series of small accords which, taken together, pave the way for the ultimate resolution.

Similarly, viewing what appears to be a seemingly unitary issue as divisible — he takes one part, you another — is often the key to resolving deadlock.

The Settlement Terms

Here are some thoughts on the terms of the settlement.

Start with a reasonable offer. Don't highball (or lowball) it. You can get a reasonable dialogue going only if you show you mean business.

On the other hand, it's foolish to start with your best offer, even if you label it as such and ooze sincerity. Your adversary won't believe you. Besides, he wants the satisfaction of seeing you move in his direction.

Give a reason for any proposal you make. Show the other side how you arrived at it. Your adversary will have a different number, to be sure; but if you can get him to explain the rationale for his number, then there will be some basis for moving the numbers closer together. It's easier to argue about rationales than about numbers.

To reach a deal, the plaintiff has to come in with a number that he has a good chance of topping if he takes the case to trial — so that the defendant's lawyer would need to explain to his client *after* the trial why the proposal wasn't accepted. The defendant's offer, in turn, must force the plaintiff's counsel to tell his client that the court might well grant less, or not enough more to warrant the risks and expenses of trial and the delays in getting his money — i.e., that it's a fair price for removing uncertainty.

Don't bid against yourself. Find out your adversary's number before sweetening your offer.

If you go into a negotiating session with a number and suffuse it with appropriate rationale, don't change the number at the same session. Stick for that day, at least.

Once you get into the bargaining, don't make a myriad of small concessions. A lesser number of meaningful concessions encourages the other side to reciprocate. And each number should have its own rationale; be sure to tell your adversary how you arrived at your new stopping point.

When the bidding starts to get close, slow down on "splitting the difference," which changes your position without any commitment on the part of the other side to the intermediate figure.

Finally, keep cool. As settlement nears and the tension builds, minor points often tend to be magnified way out of proportion. Don't get caught up in your client's ego or his indignation. As George Jean Nathan said, "No one can think clearly when his fists are clenched." In a litigious world, it takes a cool head to resolve hot disputes.

THE OUTER LIMITS OF PRINCIPLED BARGAINING

Those are my principles; and if you don't like them, I have others."

–Groucho Marx

How would you classify yourself as a negotiator? Try this test. When you get involved in striking a deal or resolving a dispute:

- Do you view the participants as
  a. *adversaries, or*
  b. *problem-solvers?*

- Is your goal
  a. *victory, or*
  b. *a wise outcome, reached efficiently and amicably?*

- Do you
  a. *make threats, or*
  b. *explore interests?*

- Are you insistent
  a. *on your position, or*
  b. *on using objective criteria?*

- Do you
  a. *apply pressure, or*
  b. *attempt to reason on the basis of principle?*

If your answers were all in the (a) column, then you're probably a bargainer of the old school — an evolutionary product of haggling in Turkish bazaars and knockdown, drag-out labor/management tussles. Truly competitive bargainers hate to give an inch — digging in to their positions, demanding concessions, distrusting others, misleading opponents as to their bottom line, trying to win a contest of wills.

If you ended up each time in the (b) column, then you've probably read "Getting to Yes" by Roger Fisher and William Ury (Houghton Mifflin, 1981), which has become the bible for those who shun positional bargaining, adopt a cooperative mode, and "negotiate on the merits."

ALTERNATING APPROACHES

If you're like me, you're located somewhere in between a strictly (a) or (b) approach — sometimes slugging it out, sometimes searching for answers; one minute, trying to get a leg up, and the next, attempting to break an impasse. Particular deals or disputes — and even particular sessions within an extended negotiation — may tilt more in one direction than the other, depending on the issues involved, your adversary, your client, their respective positions, what hour it's getting to be, whether your lower back is giving you trouble, and so on.

In writing and lecturing on the subject, I've consistently adopted a sort of balance theory — that roughly half of what you do is to gain an advantage over the opposition and the other half consists of working out accommodations. So, for instance, you have to be persistent, but you also need perspective (you can't win 'em all). It's a personal approach that goes back to before Fisher and Ury did their thing (but after the Turks did theirs).

Anyway, up to now I've never bothered to develop an analytical basis for deciding which approach to use at any particular moment. But I may recently have found the key.

LEARNING FROM THE STUDENTS

Here's the background. I've been teaching a course at Fordham Law School on negotiating. A number of the students in my class, which meets at night, hold daytime jobs. Having one foot in the world of academe and the other in commerce makes for an interesting student profile. I find that not only can the students probe and analyze in the best law school tradition, but they also have plenty of practical know-how — street smarts — in dealing with such business affairs as negotiation.

I've been exposing the class to both the competitive and cooperative approaches to bargaining. My usual technique is to pose a hypothetical negotiating situation, and then get the students to address the key issues in terms of various tacks the bargainers might take.

In one recent class, the overall topic was resolving disputes (as contrasted with striking a deal). As a lawyer who spends most of his time doing deals but has lately gotten involved in several cases of dispute resolution, I had been struck by the differences between the two setups — the brooding presence of the litigation alternative in a dispute (as contrasted with a simple walkaway in a deal), the uncertainty of a judicial result, the heightened emotions of a legal scrap, the mood of distrust between the parties, their ambivalence over suing or settling, the rigidity caused by each side's fear of showing weakness, and the frequent absence of a problem-solving mentality

— all of which make resolving a dispute so difficult (as seen in the prior essay, "Bridging Troubled Waters").

In short, it's a fertile field for application of the Fisher-Ury technique.

THE GROOM AND THE TENT MAN

So, here's the situation I gave the class that evening — not a hypothetical scene but a vignette from real life.

In January 1985, I got married. The wedding party was held in our new apartment, occupying the two lower floors of a brownstone in New York City. In order to have enough room for a sit-down dinner, we hit on the idea of using our small garden in the back of the house.

Now, this required a large tent and sufficient heat to overcome the wintry weather. The tent man came, surveyed the scene, and said, "no problem"; with two large heaters (which he would supply), it would be perfectly comfortable. His price was, let's say, $500.

Early on the day of the wedding, the tent man and his people installed the tent. He showed the caterer how to operate one of the large gas heaters. I asked the tent man to test the second heater; he declined, saying they had just tested it back at their place, where it worked fine; and he left.

When the caterer tried to start the heaters a few hours before the party, the second heater refused to function. He tried everything, but to no avail. Repeated calls to the tent man were unanswered. The single heater was not sufficient to overcome the winter's chill. No one sat in the garden; and though the party was a good one, things were really crowded in the house.

Well, I told the class, you can imagine how furious my wife and I were — our feelings aggravated, naturally, by it being our wedding day, when everything was supposed to go smoothly. We promptly took the only step plausible under the circumstances: We stopped payment on the tent man's check! And that, of course, made him equally furious.

BLUSTERING VS. THE HIGH ROAD

So, the stage was set, either for some hard competitive bargaining over whether we ought to pay for all or a portion of the rental — bargaining that was sure to be influenced by the emotions of the moment — or possibly for a different, more rational kind of approach to this knotty situation.

First, I had the class try out some tactics of the blustering variety. Students, simulating the tent man, cast aspersions on the technological competence of our caterer, suggested that my relatives were too lily-livered to take a little cool weather, and demanded every penny of the original rental. Other students, in the roles of my bride and me, were totally self-righteous, refusing to pay a red cent ("We didn't get a single minute's use out of that tent!"), insinuating that the heater had never been checked, moaning about the pain and suffering we had undergone starting off our married life in such cramped quarters.

Then, I talked in general terms about the "Getting to Yes" approach — particularly the chapter entitled "Separate the People from the Problem," which had been part of their assignment. Put yourself in the other person's shoes; see the situation as he sees it. Don't always place the worst interpretation on what your adversary does. Recognize his need to save face — to reach agreement without seeming to back down. Identify the emotions that

are there; acknowledge your opponent's concerns as legitimate; tell him how *you* feel, rather than throwing stones. And ultimately, think of yourselves as partners in a side-by-side search for a fair agreement, advantageous to both parties.

All right, I said to the class; now, let's try to apply this approach to the tent situation. Assume that you're the tent man meeting with my wife and me to see if things can be resolved without having to bring a lawsuit for the tent rental. You can expect that feelings are running high on the Freunds' part. What things could you do — things that Roger Fisher would be proud of — to help your case?

There was a lot of response. The students rose to the occasion, putting all the right words in the tent man's mouth:

"Gee, Mrs. Freund, I can understand how frustrated you must have felt. . . ."

"What an unfortunate occurrence to have happened on your wedding day. . . ."

"You probably think I never even tested the heater. . . ."

"I can certainly see why you wouldn't consider it fair to pay the full rental for the tent. . . ."

"Try for a minute to see this from my perspective. . . ."

And they were full of ideas for an imaginative solution to the dispute:

"If you pay the full rental this time, I'll be happy to let you have the tent for your next party at half-price. . . ."

"I'm really interested in your recommending my tents to your friends and neighbors, so, if you could just cover my expenses. . . ."

"I'd be happy to give you a credit for the portion of the rental applicable to the non-working heater. . . ."

In short, they joined eagerly in the search for a fair and just solution to this dispute.

NO COOPERATIVE APPROACH FOR FREUND

Then, I said, okay, now put yourself in my place, and apply the Fisher-Ury approach to my dealings with the tent man.

I waited for some insights, but the class was not responsive. There were a few half-hearted tries —

"I realize you wanted *those heaters to work. . . ."*

"I'm sure you incurred considerable expense setting up the tent. . . ."

But their hearts didn't seem to be in it. Were they having difficulty putting themselves in my shoes? Had I come across as such a competitive bargainer that they couldn't visualize me embracing the "Getting to Yes" philosophy?

I remarked on this disparity, and just to make sure I wasn't imagining things, I called for a show of hands. How many of you, I asked, favor a cooperative approach for the tent man? A substantial majority raised their hands. How many would take a cooperative approach in my shoes? Only a few hands went up.

Well, imagine that! I chortled. What's the reason? Now, the class didn't hesitate. "You've got the money!" said one student. "If the tent man is going to get some of it from you, he's got to overcome your negative feelings."

"That's right," added another. "It would be different, if you had paid in cash. Then *you* might have had to search for mutual interests — assuming you didn't want to throw good money after bad by initiating suit. But here, you're sitting pretty; you can afford to take a hard-nosed position."

For a third student, the real difference lay in the tent man's being at fault — his heater didn't work and he wasn't even reachable by phone. That responsibility made it more logical for the tent man to adopt a "come, let us reason together" approach; whereas I — blameless under the circumstances — didn't have to reach as far.

"But wait," another student cautioned, "all we've heard is *your* side of the story!" And, of course, he was absolutely right. I had set forth the facts accurately, but perhaps a bit loaded in my direction. For example, my crucial premise for paying nothing was that the non-working heater had rendered the tent completely unusable; an argument might have been made that it had *some* utility (e.g., for storing food and equipment).

Another student pointed out that since the tent man was operating an ongoing business, there might be opportunities to rent to me (or my friends or neighbors) in the future, which could influence him to take a less dogmatic approach. I, on the other hand, could just as easily walk my fingers through the Yellow Pages in search of a more reliable alternative.

And finally, several of the students focused on the difficulties and expenses the tent man would have in bringing an action, including the presumption that the court's sympathy would be on the side of the newlyweds.

WHO'S GOT THE MARBLES?

It didn't surprise me that a majority of the class thought the tent man ought to use the Fisher approach —

that's exactly what I would have utilized in his place to get that hard-nosed Freund to come down off his high horse and at least cover the installation expenses. But I was taken aback that so few people thought *I* ought to. Maybe I shouldn't have been — although "Getting to Yes" doesn't make these kinds of distinctions. I had the money, he was at fault, and litigation wasn't a desirable alternative. In that situation, they were saying, why should I bend over backward to accommodate the other side?

I tinkered with some of the variables. Would the students be more disposed (as me) to bargain on principle had I paid cash, and now wished to get back my money, or at least some of it? I think clearly they would have been.

The significance of where the money resided was not lost on them. (Earlier in the evening, I had asked them whether they thought I ought to let the tent man in to pick up his tent the next day. Of course, of course, they all said — it would be dirty pool on my part to hang onto the tent, if not outright conversion. But when I changed the facts to my having paid *cash,* a lot of them weren't too sure; perhaps hanging onto the property — a little self-help — *would* be called for in that circumstance.)

Now, it's too simplistic to conclude from this that whenever your cause is just and you're holding the money, you can afford to hang tough — that cooperative bargaining has no appeal for you under those circumstances. In fact, there's almost always some cost to persons on *either* side of a dispute; the equities are rarely the exclusive province of one party; there may be real value in sustaining a relationship; and litigation is no fun for anybody but court reporters.

So, even with the strongest of cases, I might still be receptive to a reasoned approach from the other side (except possibly on my wedding day or when I've had root canal work); and while I'd put a pretty price on my willingness to settle, I could see myself cooperating to arrive at that point.

But — and here's the real lesson I learned from my students — if I'm sitting there with all the marbles, I'll be damned if I'm going to *initiate* the principled approach! And when some unrepentant tent man comes blustering in demanding his money, he's not going to get any come-let-us-reason-together pap from this old bird!

NEGOTIATION JUJITSU

One of Roger Fisher's colleagues told me that the tent man example illustrates when positional bargaining is most useful; i.e., where there is a strong alternative to a negotiated agreement (here, holding the cash, paying nothing and waiting to be sued), and where the transaction is single-issue (money), two-party, single-shot and without important or ongoing personal or institutional relationships. A well-rounded negotiator, he said, should be able to be a good positional bargainer when the situation calls for it.

As a matter of fact, one guy who probably *wouldn't* have been surprised at the class's outcome is Roger Fisher. He has actually included a chapter in his book entitled, "What If They Won't Play?" This situation must come up a lot; you're trying to discuss interests while the guy on the other side is stating his position in unequivocal terms, attacking your proposals (or even you), and concerned only with maximizing his own gains. How do you get him to focus on the merits?

Roger's answer: use *negotiation jujitsu.* Avoid the cycle of action and reaction; sidestep the other side's attack and deflect it against the problem — as in the Oriental martial arts, where you use your skill to turn the opponent's strength to your ends. This involves such methods as treating your adversary's position as one possible option — looking for the interests that lie behind it, seeking out the principle it reflects, considering ways to improve it — as well as inviting the other side's criticism of your ideas (so you can rework them in light of what you learn from their negative judgments), and recasting any personal attacks on you as an attack on the problem. Two of the key techniques advocated are asking questions instead of making statements (statements generate resistance, whereas questions generate answers), and using silence — creating the impression of a stalemate that the other side will feel compelled to break by coming up with a new suggestion.

It's too bad the tent man didn't read "Getting to Yes." I can just picture him now.

"Yes sir, Mr. Freund, I can certainly see that your not paying a red cent is one of the possible options here. . .[Pause]. . .Do you really think, though, that it would be a just settlement of the problem?. . .[Silence]. . .I'd be interested in understanding how you believe calling me an 'incompetent idiot' gets us closer to a solution of this matter. . .[Pained smile]. . .What, if I may ask, are some of your objections to my position that you should pay the full rental plus interest for the month that has now passed?. . .[Listen]. . . ."

WELL, WHAT HAPPENED?

Anyway, you're probably wondering what actually happened. After a quick round of mutual recriminations, the tent man turned the matter over to a collection agency, which wrote a very nasty letter. I turned the letter over to one of my litigation partners, who wrote a blistering reply. The collection agency wrote again, completely ignoring the reply and demanding payment. My partner once again responded, this time hinting at dire happenings (a treble-damage suit for pain and suffering? Perhaps RICO. . .) if this harrassment continued. After that, I never again heard from the collection agency. A year later, my wife and I happily celebrated our first anniversary — indoors, of course.

LYING IN NEGOTIATIONS

Recently, I was representing a public company that was in the process of being acquired — not entirely of its own volition. Negotiations over price and other key subjects were hot and heavy, but on price the purchaser wasn't giving an inch. At a crucial point, the purchaser's investment banker asked me point-blank whether we had another corporate buyer for the company.

In fact, though there had been nibbles, we had no other corporate buyer. To reply that one existed would have been a lie. I couldn't do it — even though the purchaser might well have felt the need to increase his price with an active corporate rival in the field.

On the other hand, to reply in the negative would provide important information to my adversary — information that would undoubtedly strengthen his stand on price. So I bobbed and weaved as best I could, mumbling something like, "We're not without options, I can assure you, but I'm not at liberty to disclose what they are" — and then, a little later, "Hey, would you like to wake up tomorrow morning and find out the company has been sold?"

At any rate, my responses had little effect; the other side didn't budge. And since nothing else materialized, my client ultimately had to take what was offered.

"Well... Do you have another buyer?"

"Why, of course we do!"

THE PREVALENCE OF
MISREPRESENTATION

Reflecting on the incident that night, I wondered whether my scruples were old-fashioned. The fact is, a great deal of lying goes on daily at negotiating tables across the land — and not just by non-lawyers. People may use euphemisms to describe their conduct, but what it really comes down to is one side attempting to mislead the other in order to gain an advantage.

In past writings on this subject, I drew a distinction between a misrepresentation of fact (which was a real "no-no") and what I termed "creative motivation" — the phony rationale negotiators sometimes offer as to why their client can't make a certain warranty or to back up the suggested addition of a particular provision to the contract (the idea being that, if they served up the *real* reason unvarnished, their adversary would never concede the point). While I didn't encourage ∙dissembling about motive, I felt it was widespread and generally condoned on the theory that the other side wasn't entitled to see the inner workings of your mind. Therefore, take nothing at face value, I warned negotiators; examine closely every ostensible rationale.

I realize now that this distinction didn't cut deep enough. Lots of *facts* are misrepresented, too. The more meaningful distinction may be between which facts should be sacrosanct and which lend themselves to various forms of disguise. More on that later.

INFORMATION BARGAINING

The issue of deception in negotiations is one aspect of what's termed "information bargaining." Information is crucial to a negotiator: The more he has, the more confident he can be about such matters as what price will swing the deal, which arguments will persuade, what promises are meaningful. The information may relate directly to what's being bought or sold, or to the seriousness of a proposition, or may concern the party himself (in terms of his authority or intentions).

Good negotiators plan ahead, outlining the information they seek and initiating a series of informal probes to elicit it. They often begin with open-ended questions, turning more specific in the follow-up phase, and always *listening* — there's no telling what goodies may come your way if you shut up and let the other guy talk for a while.

NEEDS FUNDS; LACKS NIBBLES

Let's examine the issues of information and deception in a simple hypothetical situation. Mr. Cellar is selling his house; Ms. Byre would very much like to buy it. Cellar starts out asking $200,000. Byre wants to make a deal at around $175,000, but is prepared to go as high as $190,000. She offers $150,000. Cellar pooh-poohs Byre's offer and doesn't budge. Byre violates the precept of not bidding against oneself and raises her offer to $160,000. Cellar still hangs tough but hints that he might be willing to knock $10,000 off his asking price.

Now, consider the significance to the bargaining of the following information. Assume that Ms. Byre knew for sure that (1) Mr. Cellar had already bought another house, was very close to closing, and needed funds from the sale of his existing home to pay for the new one; and (2) although there have been some nibbles, Cellar has no other ready, willing, and able buyer for his existing home at the moment. Clearly, this would give Ms. Byre a leg up in the ensuing negotiations; she might well be able to pressure Cellar into her $175,000 range by playing a little hardball.

On the other hand, if for all intents and purposes Cellar is in no particular rush to dispose of his home (with no need for funds on the horizon), and several other buyers are actively bidding for the property, then Byre might consider it necessary to strike an immediate deal with Cellar at the $190,000 level just to make sure she gets the house of her dreams.

If Cellar is savvy, he'll also understand these dynamics. He wouldn't want Byre to know about his need for immediate cash, and he realizes she'll be tempted to fold rather than negotiate if she's worried about other purchasers.

Cellar might even go to some lengths to suggest the existence of the latter. Let's say his phone rings while Ms. Byre is at the house. Cellar picks it up and listens for a minute. Then, in a stage whisper loud enough for Byre to overhear, he says, "Well, I've got someone else here looking at the house right now, but you could come over at 4 p.m." — implying, without stating, that another buyer is on the line (though, in fact, it's his neighbor, calling to arrange a good time for returning a borrowed lawn mower).

PROBING FOR INFORMATION

Now, Byre should probe a bit on these two issues (whether Cellar needs funds and whether he has other nibbles) to find out whatever she can. This calls for an informal approach, so as not to put Cellar on his guard that he's about to surrender any information of real value. She might say, "This sure is a lovely place. Have you

found a comparable new one yet?" Or perhaps she might
ask whether any of this furniture is for sale — the answer
could be a tip-off. She could try to glean information from
the broker about whether this house is a hotbed of other
prospective purchasers. Or Cellar himself might let the
cat out of the bag by noting that he'll insist on a quick
closing.

If all else fails, there's always the direct question: "Do
you need the proceeds from this transaction to pay for
your new home?" "Is anyone else bidding on the house
right now?" (Note: This latter form is preferable to
saying, "Look, I *know* you don't have another purchaser. . ." — which is easy to evade by the reply, "Don't be
so sure.")

CONTRACT AND TORT ACTIONS

Assume now that the bargaining is occurring between
the *attorneys* for Cellar and Byre and that these very
questions are posed by Byre's lawyer to Cellar's lawyer.
Further assume that Cellar's lawyer knows that the
truthful answers are "yes" (Cellar needs the proceeds),
and "no" (there are no other bidders), respectively. The
ethical issue is squarely posed.

First, let's analyze the legal and ethical context for
Cellar's lawyer. (I've not done any independent research
on the subject but have drawn on material contained in
several articles on the subject.[1])

---

[1] James J. White, "Machiavelli and the Bar: Ethical Limitations on
Lying in Negotiations," 4 American Bar Association Research Journal
926 (1980); Thomas F. Guernsey, "Truthfulness in Negotiations," 17
University of Richmond Law Review 99 (1982); and Rex R. Persch-
bacher, "Regulating Lawyers' Negotiations".)

Lawyers who misrepresent in negotiations run some risks under established principles of contract and tort law. In oversimplified terms, if the negotiator makes an affirmative misrepresentation of fact that is fraudulent or material and induces the recipient to make the contract, and if the recipient's reliance on the misrepresentation is justified, then the injured party may void his contract.

Under certain circumstances, there may even be a duty to speak. For example, if a negotiator has previously made an honest assertion that is no longer true, he has an obligation to correct it. And if he obtains a competitive advantage through unethical or dishonest practices — a buyer's representative, for example, who learns of valuable mineral deposits on the seller's land by secretly trespassing on it — that knowledge must be disclosed.

Misrepresentations can also form the basis for a damage action in tort against the maker; but here, along with the other elements, the misrepresentation must be both fraudulent *and* material. The negotiator is not relieved from liability because he acts in a representative capacity (unless his client has lied to him); and the client is subject to liability for most of the negotiator's misrepresentations (whether authorized or not).

THE ETHICAL FRAMEWORK

These rules affect *all* negotiators. In addition, *lawyers* are subject to certain ethical rules concerning negotiation. While courts have been reluctant to use ethical rules as a basis for imposing civil liability on lawyers for the benefit of third parties, attorneys have been disciplined in a number of cases for making factual misrepresentations to third parties.

The Model Rules of Professional Conduct deal with this area in general terms, providing (in Model Rule 4.1) that lawyers shall not knowingly make a false statement of fact or law to third parties or knowingly fail to disclose a fact to a third party when such failure is equivalent to misrepresentation. But the concept of truthfulness is an elusive one, on which consensus is notably lacking.

You see, the real problem here is the classic paradox facing all negotiators, which one of the commentators summed up in these candid terms:

> "On the one hand the negotiator must be fair and truthful; on the other hand he must mislead his opponent. Like the poker player, a negotiator hopes that his opponent will overestimate the value of his hand. Like the poker player, in a variety of ways he must facilitate his opponent's inaccurate assessment. . . . To conceal one's true position, to mislead an opponent about one's true settling point, is the essence of negotiation."

DRAWING THE LINE

So, where should the line be drawn? I think we would all agree that lawyers can (and often do) strongly advocate weakly held views about the meaning of a decision or statute — arguing for plausible interpretations that favor their client's interest, even if they're not personally convinced. Similarly, distortion concerning the value of one's case (or other subject matter of the negotiation) — puffery, if you will — is part of the game. And the bargaining demand about which the bargainer cares little — placed on the table to increase his supply of negotiating currency — while not a commendable practice, doesn't shock the conscience.

These cases are relatively easy, because as one commentator puts it, the rules of the game are explicit and well-developed in such areas. Everyone expects a lawyer to distort the value of his own case and overstate his arguments while depreciating those of his adversary; the system accepts this behavior and allows certain widely used ploys that aren't deemed morally reprehensible.

On the other hand, notwithstanding this latitude, the authorities state that a lawyer may not assert as a transactional fact (a fact related to the situation being negotiated) anything that he knows is not true or anything that cannot reasonably be inferred from the information available to him.

THE ETHICAL DILEMMA

Now, let's go back to Cellar's lawyer. The questions posed to him relate to matters that are collateral to the subject matter, albeit important. They don't go to the quality of what's being sold and bought; rather, they relate to the bargaining of the parties — the need to sell quickly, the availability of other alternatives. They're just the kind of facts that in my experience most often pose the ethical dilemma.

Let's say that Cellar's lawyer blatantly lies, inventing another buyer who is ready to pay $180,000 on the spot. On learning of this, Ms. Byre panics and concludes an immediate deal at $190,000. After the closing, she learns of the misrepresentation. Would she have a valid cause of action?

Well, the representation was of a fact; it was clearly fraudulent; it induced her to make the contract; and particularly since a lawyer was doing the talking, I would think that her reliance on the statement was justified. So, a contract claim is made out, and she may well be able to void her agreement (which, on our facts, she probably wouldn't want to do!).

As for a tort claim against the lawyer or his client, it would be necessary for her to prove also that the misrepresentation was material. Clearly it seemed so to her; but since the fact misrepresented was collateral to the basic transaction, a court might not consider it so. Even if liability were established, how would damages be assessed? There appear to be few reported cases in this area.

On the ethical point, at least one commentator has interpreted the opinions to stand for the proposition that lawyers are *not* permitted to "create" another offer to use as leverage. Thus, an untruthful answer to this question may well subject Cellar's attorney to disciplinary action.

MATTERS OF INTENTION

Now, how about the question regarding Cellar's use of the purchase price to pay for his new house? This falls more into the category of intention; and while a statement as to someone's intention does contain an assertion of fact, the issue is whether a case can be made for justifiable reliance. Lying about this sort of thing may be reprehensible, but I would have doubted that a contract or tort action could be based on it.

That is, until my attention was directed to *Chase Manhattan Bank, N.A. v. Perla*[2] in which a New York court ruled that an injured lender could sue the debtor's lawyer

---

[2] 65 A.D.2d 207, 411 N.Y.S. 2d 66 (1978).

for fraud on the basis of a statement concerning what the debtor would do in the future. According to the court, if the lawyer has knowledge that the future action will not be carried out, the statement as to the client's intention is a fraudulent misrepresentation of fact. So here, a statement by Cellar's lawyer that the proceeds of the old house will *not* be needed to close the new house — when he knows they will be — could well fall within the *Perla* ambit.

Let's look at the related area of bargaining demands that relate to the client's intention. One commentator uses the following example: A borrower is trying to borrow from a bank at least $5 million at no more than prime plus four percent interest. His lawyer tells the bank, "My client does not want to accept less than $10 million at prime plus two percent interest." While literally a truthful statement of intention — the client *doesn't want* terms worse than that, although he will accept them — it's clearly designed to mislead. Ethically, however, it does not create a problem.

Now, what if the lawyer had said, "My client *will not agree* to borrow your money unless you charge no more than prime plus two percent and lend $10 million." The statement of intention is now not only deceptive but also untruthful. Most people are aware that negotiators frequently ask for as much as they can get — but does that justify the lie? The "does not want" language was more precise (and thus literally truthful), but must excessive demands be so precise? It's a close call that clearly troubles the authorities.

In terms of false statements, the comment to Model Rule 4.1 says that what constitutes a fact "can depend on the circumstances" and goes on to state that "under generally accepted conventions in negotiation certain types of statements ordinarily are not taken as statements of facts." The examples of such conventions include estimates of price or value and a party's intentions as to an acceptable settlement.

Now, take this case from one of the articles. A defendant has instructed his lawyer to accept any settlement offer less than $100,000. Plaintiff's lawyer says, "I think $90,000 will settle this case. Will your client give $90,000?" It's a tough dilemma for the defendant's lawyer. A truthful answer concludes the negotiation and destroys any possibility of negotiating a lower settlement — even though plaintiff might well be willing to accept half of that. (Even a brief hesitation in replying might provide significant information to a sharp plaintiff's lawyer.) Yet a negative response is a lie. Is it fair to lie in this case? Is that part of the "rules of the game'? Can it be justified on the grounds that the *question* is unfair? The commentator thinks not (and recommends avoidance techniques, which are discussed below) but does not appear to be totally comfortable with his conclusion.

THE UNFAIRNESS GUIDELINE

So, what guidelines can we derive from all this? One of the commentators has suggested a helpful test: that liability for misrepresentation should depend on whether the deception causes some unfairness in the bargaining situation. Thus, the issue is not whether there's intent to deceive or mislead, but rather, whether or not the nature of the statement makes it likely that the negotiator will succeed in doing so. In this formulation, the element of justifiable reliance becomes critical. And the more specific the statement, the more likely it will be treated as a factual representation for which the negotiator may be held liable; the less specific — this case is a "real winner" or this transaction "a real steal" — the greater likelihood of it being considered mere opinion or puffing.

DON'T LIE

One thought I'd like to add to this is that lawyers should not limit their concerns to being sued or hauled before a grievance committee. A lawyer who consistently misrepresents facts in the course of negotiations — whether or not such falsehoods are actionable — develops a reputation for untrustworthiness that can be extremely harmful to his career. No short-term advantage gained through improper behavior is worth the resultant long-term ill effects.

Another thought: lying runs counter to everything we lawyers should stand up tall for. Shun it like the plague.

BLOCKING TECHNIQUES

So, what should you do when put in the position of Cellar's lawyer by that assertive attorney for Byre who wants answers? Well, there are various ways for negotiators to protect information that ought not to be divulged. After all, according to Fisher and Ury, ("Getting to Yes,"),[3] less than full disclosure is not the same thing as deliberate deception: "Good faith negotiation does not require total disclosure."

Here, according to one authority,[4] are some of the so-called blocking techniques that can be used (which I'll try to apply to the two issues in the house situation):

---

[3] Penguin Books, 1983, p. 140.
[4] Harbaugh and Britzke, "Primer on Negotiation," P.L.I., 1984.

questions generally. ("Obviously, I will have to live somewhere; I'm not about to take to the streets.")

- *Answer another question.* Give information on a related non-sensitive query. ("Funny you should ask. The broker was just saying the other day that this would be a perfect house for a doctor who has his office at home. . . .")

- *Overanswer the question.* Give all possible answers without making a commitment to any one response. ("I may have other buyers; I may have one buyer; I may have a prospective buyer. . . .")

- *Answer a question with a question.* ("Are you bidding on any other houses?")

- *Rule the question out of bounds.* ("I think my financial needs are an inappropriate, irrelevant area of inquiry.")

- *Ignore the question.* This can be done either by silence or by changing the topic. ("How do you like the icemaker on the refrigerator?")

These kinds of techniques often require advance planning; spur-of-the-moment responses may inadvertently communicate information one wants to protect.

But remember, if you use these techniques too often — if you're too evasive — your adversary may feel he's located a "soft spot" which he'll then proceed to exploit.

THE ASSERTIVE APPROACH

My own preference is to take a somewhat more aggressive tack. On the "other buyer" issue, I might say:

"I don't want to get into that. Make up your mind on the merits of the house itself. I'm telling you, it will take $200,000 to buy this house."

Or:

"I don't have a firm offer at this time. But I do have a *potential* purchaser *(assuming there is one)* who, if he decides to buy, is clearly capable of paying $200,000. Are you willing to take the risk that I'll pass up your lowball bid for the greater expectancy?"

On the "other house" and resultant need for speed, I might try this:

"I love this house. It was a wrench for me to decide to sell it. Now that I've decided, I want it to happen quickly. You're well-advised to get me signed, sealed, and delivered before I change my mind and take it off the market."

LYING VS. MISLEADING

There's one other topic I want to touch on. Let's say a lawyer is asked a factual question by the other side ("Has your client had any recent labor problems?"). The lawyer is aware that, indeed, his client has had such problems; but, it would be harmful to the lawyer's client for the other side to learn this. He replies: "I don't know." Sound familiar?

Now, clearly this is a misrepresentation (as to the state of the lawyer's knowledge) to which one shouldn't resort; more imaginative ways can be employed to block the flow of information. However, in the context of negotiations (as contrasted with judicial proceedings, where to feign lack of knowledge is not only unethical but also unforgivable), it's probably not actionable, except in special circumstances.[5]

The question I'd like to leave you with is whether or not you consider this worse than a literally truthful statement that is designed to (and does) provide the other side with misleading information (e.g., answering "yes" to the question of whether your client has a long-term lease on certain premises, when you know that he's recently received a notice from the landlord commencing eviction proceedings). The "I don't know," by contrast, is untruthful but doesn't transmit any misleading substantive information — just an absence of information, from which the recipient may draw an adverse inference, alerting him to inquire elsewhere for the facts.

I know, I know — you're saying, "Both are awful; why should I have to choose?" Just stick with me for another minute and try this test; it might reveal something about yourself. Which embarrassment would you rather endure — having your adversary discover after the fact that he was misled as to substance by a literally truthful answer that you must have known would mislead him, or that you in fact did know something that you had told him you didn't know (but without misleading him as to substance)?

I have only anecdotal evidence for my hypothesis, but I suspect your answer may well turn on the kind of work you do. For example, litigators — who worry about perjury on a daily basis and who spend hours tutoring their clients to answer only the question asked and to avoid being expansive — would probably rather endure the embarrassment of being caught in the truthful-albeit-misleading response. On the other hand, corporate lawyers — whose major professional concern under the securities laws is avoiding the misleading statement or

---

[5] *See, e.g., Slotkin v. Citizens Casualty Co. of New York,* 614 F. 2d 301 (2d Cir. 1979).

omission — may be more inclined in this dilemma to opt for the non-misleading-untruthful-lack of knowledge response. How do you come out?

ON YOUR OWN IN THE WEE HOURS

I was just dozing off on the New York to San Francisco flight when the announcement came over the loud-speaker: "Is there a *lawyer* on the plane? Please push your stewardess-call button."

That's odd, I thought. . . . But, never one to shirk responsibility, I pushed my button. The stewardess appeared.

"Oh, sir, would you please help us?" she asked. "We have a troublesome problem in the rear of the plane."

I followed her down the aisle. In the last row sat a small elderly man, staring straight ahead, his face very white.

"He's convinced he's going to die before we land," whispered the stewardess. "A doctor has checked him out but didn't find anything. The man has repeatedly asked to speak to a lawyer."

I leaned over the man. His voice was very soft. "I'm dying," he said, "and I have no will. My children will inherit my property, and I don't want them to. Can you help me?"

The last will I'd drafted was a few years out of law school, for a cousin. This definitely wasn't my area of practice. I turned to the stewardess. "Did anyone else answer your call for a lawyer?"

"No," she replied, "you're the only one. It's up to you."

I didn't hesitate. "I'm no expert," I said to the old man, 'but I'll see what I can do. Stewardess, please fetch my attaché case."

I rolled up my sleeves and went to work. With gentle but probing questions, I divined the old man's intentions. Then I drafted provisions in rapid penstrokes on my yellow pad. By visualizing the contents of my own will, I made sure all necessary subjects were covered. I was aware, of course, that serious questions of applicable law were posed, as the plane crossed over each state line; but this was no time to be plagued by self-doubt — I had to act, and I did.

As the flight passed over Omaha, the will was signed, witnessed by two stewardesses and the flight engineer, and in shape for filing in probate court.

"How can I thank you?" said the old man, tears streaming down his cheeks. "I have travelers checks. . ."

"No, no," I cut him off. "The profession has been good to me. This one," I said, striding back down the aisle to my seat, "is on the house."

"FASTEN YOUR SEAT BELTS. PLEASE EXTINGUISH ALL CIGARETTES."

The plane's p.a. system blared and I woke up with a start. The old man — the will — had it all been a dream?

THE SECRET FANTASY

Of course it had. In fact, it's probably every lawyer's secret fantasy — the exhiliration of being needed, of coming through under pressure, of easing an old man's last hours, of screwing the heirs. . . .

Unfortunately, however, in all my years of traveling on planes, going to the theatre, and attending sporting events, no one has ever intoned those magical words, "Is there a lawyer in the house?" Yet, I invariably feel a twinge of envy whenever I hear a doctor summoned by loudspeaker to play a crucial, impromptu role — pitting his skills against the grim reaper on alien turf. It has such an elemental quality. People don't seem to need lawyers in the same way.

Maybe it's just as well. Fresh out of law school, I might have been able to perform some rudimentary legal tasks for a damsel (or testator) in distress, but I'd feel awfully deficient today, operating in areas outside my own. There are so many segments of the law that I know very little about; everything is so terribly complex; and attributes like reason and logic — qualities such as common sense — won't get you very far if the issue involves, say, the Internal Revenue Code or equitable distribution.

Perhaps if there were more calls for lawyers to render emergency services, we'd be motivated to stockpile small bits of rudimentary knowledge useful on planes and in other emergency locales — you know, a legal Heimlich maneuver for each foreseeable crisis. But the absence of occasion has placed this low on our list of priorities.

It does make one wonder, though, how the physician answering that p.a. system call — a brain surgeon by profession — handles an appendectomy in the smoking section of the airliner. Either (a) these guys are much more versatile than we are, or (b) there's less complexity in crossing over from one discipline to another in medicine than in law, or (c) they manage to fake it (i) by immediately summoning an ambulance if the situation seems critical, or (ii) if things appear under control, by prescribing two aspirins and plenty of bed rest.

FUNCTIONING ON A PRIMITIVE LEVEL

At any rate, there's a different facet of this issue that's more interesting than our ability to fake it in areas outside our specialty. And that's our ability to fake it *within* our specialty!

Most of the important things we do take place in our own offices, surrounded by books of reference, awash in similar documents from other deals — with junior lawyers to call on for assistance, and other legal disciplines available at the touch of a telephone. Sure, there's pressure, but there's also enough time to touch all the bases before reaching a final, measured determination.

And *that* is the basis on which we're generally judged as professionals — just as a surgeon's reputation rises or falls on the results from the hospital operating table, not by how well he functions under the stands of the stadium.

Still, there are times as a lawyer when you're called upon to function on a more primitive level — when there's no coterie of expertise and assistance for comfort, when the business realities of the situation overwhelm the legal niceties — in short, when you're on the line.

"GET IT SIGNED!"

For me, this situation comes up most often in the context of negotiating — either to strike a deal or resolve a dispute — where the two sides, after bargaining over a sustained period, finally agree on the principal terms (like price); and now your client is determined to translate that handshake into a binding contract before the parties disperse from the table.

Why this anxiety to sign up the deal? There are various possibilities: (a) an imminent deadline for having a signed agreement (like fiscal year-end); (b) the necessity to take (or not take) some action tomorrow, as to which the outcome of these negotiations is directly relevant; (c) your client's (or your own) lack of trust in dealing with the adversary; or (d) the simple realization that people can change their minds — so it's good practice to pin things down while the mood is conciliatory.

The fact is — as every negotiator knows from bitter experience — that no deal is done until it's done. So, get it done!

What really bothers the client — and rightfully so — is when he has to push his lawyer to finish the job over the lawyer's protests ("I don't have the tools — we need time — we'll leave something out."). If the client thinks it's important to sign up today, and this is possible to accomplish, then the lawyer shouldn't demur — if for no other reason than the enormous potential for second-guessing should the opportunity to commit the adversary be allowed to pass and it turns out he later welshes.

In fact, when your own client doesn't seem to grasp the need for a speedy resolution, you should advise him to press for it ("Based on my experience, I urge you: don't let that guy out of the room until he's signed on the dotted line!").

Of course, it's prudent to advise the client that this procedure involves risks — that the contract could be more definitive if you had the extra time — although, you should add (assuming it's so), you believe the risk is worth the reward. (Months later, when a gap in the agreement creates a contested issue, he may well forget your caveats — a contemporaneous file memo is always advisable — but that's the price of admission to the profession.)

'ROUND MIDNIGHT

Recently, I found myself involved in one of these situations. My specialty is mergers and acquisitions; and while I prefer to do friendly deals of the negotiated variety, I also get involved in a number of contested matters, which this was.

In brief, a dispute arose between two factions in a corporation. The controlling faction brought in a third party to buy the company; the minority faction (which I represented) opposed the terms of the deal. It looked like this would flare into open warfare — but then, all of a sudden, the parties and their lawyers were attempting to negotiate a resolution.

I hadn't fully anticipated that things would take this turn. I was in another city, far from my office, with no colleagues, no books, no forms. It was late at night. Certain events were due to happen the next day that could be materially affected by the outcome of these negotiations. As a result, both the lawyer on the other side and I considered it critical to have the parties enter into a binding agreement before dawn.

So I found myself, after midnight, alternating between negotiating, drafting, reviewing, and revising a somewhat unusual agreement (certainly not to be found in any book of forms) involving many millions of dollars — an agreement, moreover, which was likely to be challenged in the courts — with no help, under great pressure, and growing increasingly tired as the night wore on. For me, this was the functional equivalent of treating heart stoppage at Philharmonic Hall.

TIPS FOR A TIGHT SPOT

I came away from the experience with some thoughts I'd like to pass along — a dozen tips that might prove useful if you wind up in a similar tight spot.

1. Be comfortable with contracts. It's very helpful to have a basic grasp of contracts — not so much the law, but an appreciation for the structure. I'm talking about such matters as the differences between representations, covenants, and conditions, and what tasks each of these performs; the notion that conditions can be dependent or independent, and can condition the obligations of one party or both; the distinction between contractual obligations and options, and how some apparent obligations may really be nothing more than options; the desirability of prescribing a remedy for certain breaches; and so on. Get comfortable with this kind of stuff.

2. Undertake to draft. As any negotiator worth his salt knows, when the opportunity to draft presents itself, seize it. I won't go into all the reasons here (*see Lawyering,* § 7.3.3; *Anatomy of a Merger,* § 2.3.2); suffice to say, when *you* write something, you know what it means, and you can tailor the provisions, with appropriate subtlety, to seek the protection you need while skirting around issues that present problems for your own side. Reviewing your draft at this late hour, your adversary may never know what hit him. But if *he* drafts, then you have to worry about what he's trying to put over on you by the dawn's early light — and that's a lot tougher. So, even though drafting places an extra strain on you, volunteer to do it.

3. Try to be prepared. I wasn't equipped in this instance; but if you sense that the situation might arise (and have the time), draft a rough form of agreement the day before back in the office. This gives you a real head start — and may even help to win you the drafting assignment, when you announce to your adversary that you already have something prepared. If that's not possible, at least take along some other contracts — even ones that don't deal with this particular subject matter; a review of them may suggest the desirability of including additional provisions or provide boilerplate language for, e.g., a standard separability clause.

4. Don't overreach. This *isn't* the time to begin with your toughest draft and let your adversary whittle away at it piecemeal. The hours are too short, and the vibrations are bad when you're caught in the act — "Come on, Freund; what are you trying to pull on me at 3 a.m.?"

I prefer to announce that I'm doing a down-the-middle, even-handed draft — by way of alerting my adversary that his reactions should follow the same equitable path ("For God's sake, Smith, don't start *negotiating* with me!"). To put flesh on these bones, I make the operative provisions reciprocal where appropriate (rather than waiting for him to ask); and I also like to include some provisions that are solely for his benefit (although not harmful to my client) — just so he knows I have his best interests at heart.

5. Make reasonable concessions. When your adversary points out aspects of your draft that need changing, and he's clearly right, make the concession on the spot. You can hold back a few of the more debatable propositions for trading bait, but don't get hung up on the easy ones, if you want to inspire reciprocal reasonable behavior from the other side.

6. Watch for clinkers. Now, if your adversary gets to do the drafting, be very alert for clinkers. Scrutinize each provision, each phrase, for possible overtones or hidden meanings. Assume that your adversary is just as devious a draftsman as you would have been had you gotten the chance!

7. Don't nitpick. Concentrate on the major points of disagreement you have with your adversary's draft. Avoid stylistic comments or revisions of little significance, which may show how smart you are but don't add anything of substance. (In the eyes of most clients, lawyers who nitpick at moments like this — when they should be focusing on the main event — really *aren't* so smart.)

8. Be creative in compromising. There's no time for an extended impasse here, except on a real deal-breaker. Lesser issues, however thorny, have to be resolved. Don't depend on the other guy to do it. Think creatively.

Here's the quintessential compromise model. Assume a provision you've drafted states that if certain things happen (implicitly including both A and B), the result is X. Your adversary disagrees, and says the result should be Y. The two of you are at loggerheads. Bingo! — the compromise: if A happens, then X results; if B happens, then Y results. But you have to *see* it — you have to realize how seemingly indivisible issues can be split into segments to be dealt with separately.

9. Make it clear. Make sure the contractual provisions are drafted with clarity. It's so easy for ambiguity to creep in. (Of course, there are instances where you may want to be *deliberately* ambiguous — but that's another story. . . .) Clarity doesn't come easy late at night, when the thoughts are tumbling out of your head and onto the paper. Pretend you're the judge who's being called upon to construe the document. What would he want to know about the parties' real intentions? You may decide to include an interpretative provision in the agreement — in effect, telling the judge what you're trying to achieve, so that where doubt exists, each provision should be construed with this goal in mind.

10. Examine the possibilities. In addition to being clear, make sure each contract provision applies to a variety of possible eventualities. The fact that it handles the circumstance that inspired the provision isn't enough; how does it fare if something else occurs? Try to envision other fact situations against which to test the applicability of each provision.

11. The supporting cast. Once the major points are in place, the next concern is with the supporting cast. What provisions must be included to buttress the main items? For instance, should the other side be making certain representations about the subject matter? Are there appropriate collateral undertakings? What conditions to various obligations should be expressed?

12. What else? The toughest chore is trying to figure out what subjects that haven't been dealt with, should be. We can handle what's in front of us pretty well, but it's much more difficult to think about what we haven't thought of. The lawyer's constant fear is: What have I left out?

When you reach this point, my advice is to leave the room. Give yourself a chance to think, free of the pressures of adversaries and clients, unencumbered by prior drafts. What *could* happen? Is it provided for? Try to visualize other contracts you've negotiated — what issues were dealt with in those?

Finally, be sure to involve your client in the process. Ask them what factual situations they can envision arising — what business exigencies may transpire — that they would want protection against? You can't expect them to do your job for you, but this may at least avoid the "How-could-you-not-have-provided-for-that-obvious-situation?" round of second-guessing after the fact.

Oh, yes, Number 13 — make sure there's plenty of black coffee available.

*   *   *

Well, I hope you're inspired and ready to do battle. Back to basics; no more word processors and photocopied provisions; no more battalions of lawyers — no more opinion committees. . . .

You're like an Air Force colonel, rejecting the intricate teamwork of computers and missile launchers, harking back to World War I. . . . There he is, flying his Spad over enemy territory, one-on-one against the Boche, no support systems, only his wits as a guide. A sudden burst of gunfire, a yank on the throttle —

"FASTEN YOUR SEAT BELTS. PLEASE EXTINGUISH ALL CIGARETTES. . . ."

THE VEGAS RESOLUTION

In a recent deal I was negotiating, the parties were close to agreement on the purchase price. But, as so often happens, the protracted give and take that led up to this point had caused a hardening of their bargaining arteries. Each party had characterized his last few positions as final — "This is as far as I'll go under any circumstances"; they were, in effect, hoisted by their own petards. That last mile seemed too long a journey for either side to walk.

That, at least, was their public posture. In reality, it wasn't the case at all. The deal was virtually begging to be done, and both parties wanted it badly.

A PRETTY CLOSE SPREAD

To make the situation more concrete, let's say that at this point the potential buyer was offering $50 million to purchase a company, while the seller was holding out for $51 million — a two percent spread between the bid and the asked. In the corporate acquisition arena, that's a pretty tight market. And in most such cases, underneath the bluster, both sides ultimately are willing to compromise somewhere in the middle.

(In fact, when the differential represents that small a percentage of the deal, it's not unusual for one side to swallow hard and agree to the other side's number — at least if there's a face-saving way to handle the capitulation

— which is what often happens when one party won't budge and the other grows impatient.)

Achieving that final compromise, however, isn't always a piece of cake. Sure, I'm aware of the advice from negotiating mavens — try to reconcile interests rather than compromise positions, separate the people from the problem, invent options that creatively reconcile differing interests — but for better or worse, the key tactical decision here usually is: Who's going to suggest splitting it down the middle? If you wait for the other guy to make a move, it might never happen. If you do it yourself, you run a real risk.

Let's say the buyer suggests splitting the difference at $50.5 million. If the seller doesn't accept, then the buyer's implicit new position (regardless of what caveats he announces) is $50.5 million; i.e., the seller *knows* that the buyer is willing to go that far. Meanwhile, the seller is still at $51 million, and he may refuse to budge at this time. Then, if a compromise ultimately results, it's more likely to be in the neighborhood of $50,750,000 than the half-way point desired by the buyer.

In these situations, it would be helpful to have a neutral observer who could recommend splitting the differences without causing either side to change position — but no one fitting that description is likely to be around. If the lawyer tries it, or the investment banker, or anyone identified with a party, the other side probably will assume that the proposal has been pre-cleared with the client, even if the disclaimer attempts to point in the other direction (as, for instance, "It just occurred to me that perhaps I could sell my client on a number somewhere in the middle if you are willing to make a similar effort with yours. . . .") — and the damage is done.

So, although we were very close, I was worried. Reason doesn't always prevail; deals can founder, even at this point.

MY REVERIE

At home that night, I had a reverie about how this type of impasse could be resolved if the seller and buyer were both from Las Vegas. It involved a pair of dice.

I don't know if you've ever patronized a crap table, or are otherwise familiar with those little black-and-white cubes that roll across the green felt. No matter; it's really a matter of mathematics — the simple math of crap-shooting.

Each die is numbered from one to six. Two dice can produce 36 possible combinations, which translate into eleven possible numerical totals, ranging from two to 12. The most common number — seven — can be made six different ways (6- 1, 5-2, 4-3, 3-4, 2-5, 1-6); so, with 36 possibilities, the odds against the dice coming up seven on a single roll are six to one. The next most common numbers, six and eight, each can be rolled five ways. The five and nine have four variants; the four and ten, three; the three and 11, two; while "snake eyes" (two) and "boxcars" (12) have one each.

The notion was that the negotiators would link the final purchase price to a roll of the dice.

THE HARD WAYS

With the dice producing 11 possible totals, an increment of purchase price could be assigned to each number. For example, since two is the lowest total, that could serve as the low end of the bargaining range, $50 million. The highest total is 12; that would be the top of the range, $51 million. Now, it just so happens that each number in between can be assigned a $100,000 increment. (Whatever the bargaining gap, dividing it by ten creates the appropriate increments; e.g., with a $500,000 gap, the increments are $50,000 each.)

Here's a table that shows the purchase price assignments, the number of ways each total can be rolled, and the resulting odds on a single roll.

Dice Total	Purchase Price	Ways to roll (out of 36 Possibilities)	Odds Against
2	$50.0 million	1	35-1
3	$50.1 million	2	17-1
4	$50.2 million	3	11-1
5	$50.3 million	4	8-1
6	$50.4 million	5	6.2-1
7	$50.5 million	6	5-1
8	$50.6 million	5	6.2-1
9	$50.7 million	4	8-1
10	$50.8 million	3	11-1
11	$50.9 million	2	17-1
12	$51.0 million	1	35-1

As the table shows, the numbers five through nine, which relate to prices from $50.3 million through $50.7 million, account for 24 out of 36 possible combinations. In other words, the chances that a roll would fall somewhere in this midstream are two out of three. And the likelihood of an aberrational result could be minimized by providing for several rolls and averaging the results. . . .

Well, just about this time, my daydream was interrupted by the telephone. It was the lawyer on the other side, suggesting that we get together to "see if we can do something about this impasse." I was delighted; he'd blinked, and I knew how to take it from there.

But just for fun — and also because the intellectual exercise reveals interesting facets of the negotiating process — let's think through some ramifications of a gambling compromise.

WHOSE IDEA IS IT?

At the outset, *someone* would have to propose the roll, so the first issue is to figure out the likely impact on the proponent. What happens to the buyer who springs this on a seller? Would it be viewed as a signal that the buyer is willing to pay top dollar, $51 million — not just $50.5 million, as would be the case with a suggestion to split the difference? If so, this might tempt the seller (particularly if he also happened to be a poker player!) to hold firm at his price, in hopes that the buyer will ultimately come around.

That risk is definitely there. And the proposal would be advisable if the buyer had attached great significance to his last offer — the kind of thing that you hear in a lot of corporate deals, such as, "I'll go to $50 million, which is the absolute limit of the authority I have from my board of directors."

In other cases, however, this risk could be reduced substantially by the manner in which the buyer suggests the resolution. After all, there's a big difference between a buyer who's willing to pay $51 million (and it's *willingness*, not *capacity*, that's usually at issue) and a buyer who's willing to take a two percent risk that he'll have to pay $51 million — a risk with a correlative opportunity to make the purchase for $50 million. So his line should be something like, "I don't want to pay $51 million — but I'm a gambler, and if you are too, here's a way we can resolve this impasse." If the seller rejects the proposal, the buyer is still at $50 million, no matter what the seller's reading of the situation.

By the way, for some reason it seems to me easier to have the buyer make the proposal than the seller. I guess it's because both sides know that buyers are usually flexible; after all, they're clearly looking to buy. Sellers, on the other hand, often take the position that their business really isn't for sale — they're just "listening" to what the buyer has to say — so suggesting a toss of the cubes might undermine their stance of relative indifference.

INSPIRATION OR BUSINESS-AS-USUAL?

Try to imagine this situation with *lawyers* involved. (Not easy, I realize, since most attorneys would view these shenanigans with such disdain that the notion would never get off the ground.) In that case, I think the overture would best be handled lawyer-to-lawyer (after making sure, of course, that one's own client is prepared to go along). The posture is that you're trying it out on the other lawyer; if both of you like the idea, you then can attempt to sell it to your respective clients. This is much better than surprising an adversary with the crap-shooting concept in front of his client, where — even in the unlikely event that it appealed to the lawyer — he may well balk initially, since he doesn't know how the idea has gone over with his client.

Here's a tricky tactical decision of the lawyer. On the one hand, he increases the chances that the proposition isn't attributed to his client (thus causing less of a perceived change of position) if he appears to have made up the idea on the spot — the proverbial light bulb flashing on over his head. Of course, he then has to spend some time fussing with the various numbers — it can't flow too smoothly.

On the other hand, though the risk of it appearing prearranged is increased, the proposal stands a better chance of being accepted if handled in a way as to suggest that gaming solutions occur all the time — since most people don't like to be way out ahead of the pack. For this purpose, having a pad of printed scoresheets available would do wonders ("Another day, another roll of the dice").

REACTING TO THE DICE

What about the *recipient* of the proposal? Well, depending on his level of commitment to that last $1 million and his self-confidence, he has a variety of possible reactions, ranging from acceptance to outright rejection. For example, he could:

- Smile appreciatively, reject it politely, and comment that it suggests a deal in the middle may be appropriate ("and I'm prepared to negotiate along those lines"), without the onus of having been the first to try to break the deadlock.

- Accept the principle, but modify the idea:
  —"Let's roll three times and take an average."
  —"Let's not count the roll if the outside numbers come up; we'll just deal with five through nine" (which can lead to a non-dice split somewhere in the middle).
  —"Make the outside numbers $51 million and $50.5 million. . . ."
  —"I like the idea, but let's use *my* dice!" (Actually, the proposer can show that his dice aren't loaded by

offering to let the two stand for the *highest* number, with the other totals reversed accordingly.)

FLUNKING THE PROCESS TEST

Well, we could take the analysis further, but that's enough to illustrate the possibilities. As for the problem of resolving impasse, I'm afraid we'll just have to keep slogging that final mile — tamping down the emotions and holding the deal together until the final negotiated resolution takes place. The businessmen, the bankers and investment bankers, the lawyers and accountants who populate the corporate landscape — to say nothing of the courts and administrative agencies — aren't ready for the quick fix. We take our work (not to mention ourselves) seriously, we believe in concepts like "value," and we put great stock in the process by which buyers and sellers arrive at a deal.

This is particularly true where the negotiator represents interests other than his own, and it applies in spades where public companies are concerned. Can you picture a proxy statement, soliciting shareholders to approve the acquisition of the company, stating, "In arriving at the negotiated purchase price, the parties took into account the company's results of operations for the past five years, its net worth, present and historical marker values . . . and then rolled dice for the last $1 million"?

Or visualize the scene in the courtroom, in which the plaintiff's attorney (representing the holder of three shares of the acquired company) is cross-examining the company's president:

QUESTION: I'm sorry, I believe I must have misheard your answer to my last question.

Would you please repeat it — as loudly
as possible, so that everyone on the jury
is able to hear.

ANSWER: I said that, at this point in the negotiations, we decided to shoot craps. . . .

FANTASYLAND

Bad show. But indulge me for a final fantasy. Let's say
someone is brave (or naive) enough to go down this path.
He discloses it publicly and gets sued for being irrespon-
sible with the stockholders' money. The court delivers its
opinion:

Admittedly, the gaming conclusion to the negotiations was rather bizarre, to say the least. But the
defendant has advanced a simple justification for
his actions — it clinched the deal. I find that to be
the crucial factor, particularly since the evidence is
unclear whether, without this device, either party
would have budged. . . . Judgment for the defendant.

Following this judicial sanction, the idea of shooting
dice catches on, as a handy solution for this kind of
problem. In fact, when deals reach a certain point in the
bargaining, it becomes common for someone to suggest,
"Well, how about the Vegas Resolution?" — and no one
has to explain what it is (sort of like the Stayman
Convention in bridge). All over corporate America, guys
in pinstriped suits carry dice in their attaché cases — right
next to their calculators — just in case the opportunity
arises.

A few more years pass. Now, the lawyer proposing the Vegas Resolution doesn't even have to say anything. He just opens his case, takes out the dice, and rolls them in his palm (like Captain Queeg with his little steel balls), until the other side takes the hint.

In the end, every conference room across the land is equipped with a pair of dice, perched in the middle of the table near the pencils and yellow pads — like the doubling cube on a backgammon board. Whoever wants to suggest their use reaches out and pushes the dice toward his adversary, raising his eyebrow ever so slightly. The people on the other side exchange glances; their leader nods in agreement. A green felt pad is spread across the table. A certified public accountant (resembling one of those vote tabulators at the Academy Awards) is produced. He picks up the cubes. The seller yells "Boxcars!" The dice are thrown. . . .

It's a deal!

NEGOTIATING WITH NIKITA

I've been working on some notes for a novel. It's coming along nicely, and I thought a sneak preview might be in order.

Move over, Ken Follett, Frederick Forsyth, and Robert Ludlum — here comes Freund!

*   *   *

THE SITUATION

The action is set in the near future. Disarmament talks having failed, mutual paranoia inexorably intensifies, East and West mobilize their forces, a Libyan terrorist shoots a Liechtenstein archduke — and we're in the midst of World War III.

Arthur Leggup, a peacetime lawyer whose forte is negotiating deals, is serving as a captain in the U. S. Army. Entrusted with a secret mission behind enemy lines, he is captured by the Soviets and taken to KGB headquarters in Borscht, a Russian village near the Finnish border.

Incriminating papers are found in Leggup's wallet. From these, Nikita Comcleansky, the local KGB operative, deduces that Leggup possesses top-secret information about a daring American plan to sabotage the Stolichnaya vodka distillery — thereby causing a booze shortage that

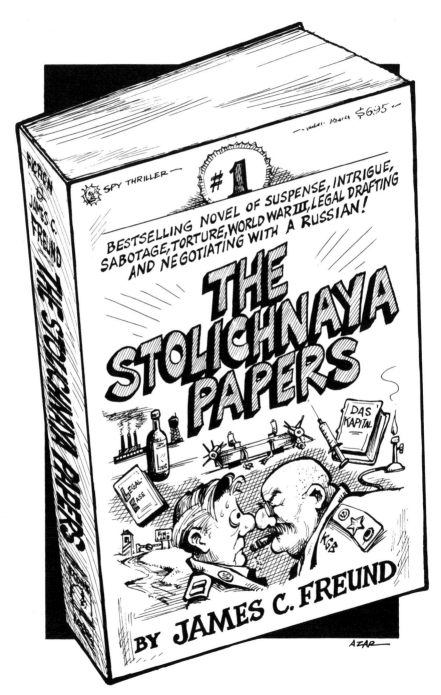

will panic the Russian populace and turn the tide of war. Comcleansky confronts Leggup, who denies knowledge of the plan. The Russian doesn't believe him and is determined to uncover the scheme.

In fact, Leggup does have the information the Reds seek. He wants desperately to remain silent but is worried that he won't be able to withstand KGB torture and will spill the beans. And Comcleansky, who resembles Ivan the Terrible, isn't making things easier:

"Tell us plan, Captain, or we be forced to pull it out by other means."

Leggup glances around uneasily. The small room is filled with electric shock devices, Bunsen burners, a medieval rack, assorted hypodermic needles, and six copies of "Das Kapital."

Suddenly, Arthur hits on a stratagem. He will attempt to negotiate with Nikita!

LET'S BARGAIN

"Just a second," says Leggup to his captor. "Let's not rush things. I've got a problem here."

"You betcha you got problem," rumbles Comcleansky, his tone menacing.

Arthur ignores the threat. "Let's assume, solely for purposes of argument, that I *do* have the information you seek. If you torture me, I won't reveal it, even though the pain be excruciating."

"You think you big hero, Captain, but let me tell you. . . ."

"On the contrary," Leggup interrupts. "The reason I wouldn't talk is because once I provide the information, you'll have no further use for me. And that's like signing my death warrant. I'm no hero; I just want to stay alive."

"You much mistaken, Captain." Comcleansky's smile is almost benevolent. "Tell us plan, and you sit out war in comfort, in very fine Soviet POW camp."

"Forgive me," says Leggup, "but I simply can't accept your verbal assurances on that point — I've seen too many World War II movies! However, if there *were* a way to provide me with an ironclad guarantee of survival, then I'd seriously consider giving you the information without the need for torture — assuming, hypothetically, that I had such information — since, all things being equal, I'm not eager to have my torso disfigured."

TWISTING THE SCREWS

What's this? Is Leggup turning traitor? Not a bit. In fact, he has concocted some realistic-sounding but unhelpful information to feed to his captors, if they rise to the bait — an "all's fair" gambit he would never stoop to in private practise. (Unfortunately, he hasn't yet figured out what to do when the Soviets discover his tale is phony. But first things first — right now, his main job is to make it out of the room with the rack.)

Well, well, Nikita Comcleansky thinks to himself, *is interesting proposition. But fast-talking Captain sounds like soldier who can't handle torture. We try a few small electric shocks, see if he cracks early.* Nikita's face glows with anticipation. *If soldier boy strong, then we pretend to cut deal with him later on. . . .*

"Wait a minute," Leggup interrupts Comcleasky's reverie. "I know what you're thinking: "Let's torture this guy a little first, just to see if he can handle it. We can always make a deal down the road.'"

— "Nyet, nyet," protests Nikita, caught in the act —

"But, you must understand, Comrade Comcleansky — I hope you don't mind if I address you by name — that if you don't negotiate with me now and instead start in with the needles, then I'll *know* you're not trustworthy. Therefore, I won't be tempted to take any deal you offer later on, because I'll be too afraid you'll welsh. Once you begin the torture, that's it. This is the only moment you have any credibility at all."

LET'S PUT IT IN WRITING

Well, Nikita isn't convinced that Leggup wouldn't still take a deal at a later point — after a few volts of electricity and a dreary chapter or two from Marx's tome — but, on the other hand, the Russian can't be sure that Arthur doesn't mean what he says. And since Leggup — unlike most of these stoic, John Wayne-type captured Americans — seems willing to provide information, Comcleansky decides it can't hurt to start down the bargaining path.

So, Nikita proposes to give Arthur a written document guaranteeing Leggup long life if he provides the desired information.

"Sorry," says Leggup, "but that's not good enough. No offense intended, Comrade, but your people haven't always treated signed agreements with total sanctity. I need something more."

Comcleansky, fuming at the national insult, whacks his bearskin gloves across Leggup's cheek. *But,* he muses, *Captain has a point.* They proceed to discuss other possible variants — including Nikita's offer to have the document countersigned by Yuri Gagarin, Olga Korbut, and the stepson of Shostakovich — but none does the trick.

THE NEUTRAL STAKEHOLDER

"I'm sorry," says Leggup, "but these written guarantees just won't do. I have an idea, though. If my geography is correct, Borscht is right near the Finnish border town of Selhinki. Finland has managed to stay neutral in the war. Why don't we get the mayor of Selhinki involved? He can act as a kind of escrow agent or third-party stakeholder. Deliver me into his custody, and then maybe we can do business."

Well, it just so happens that Comcleansky knows the mayor of Selhinki, an elderly gentleman named Paavo Mekko, from pre-war war days. Mekko is a straight shooter, meticulous in his neutrality. So, somewhat to Arthur's surprise, Nikita doesn't reject out of hand the notion of involving Mekko in some way. In fact, he sends a car to bring the mayor of Selhinki to Borscht.

Arthur is delighted; his tactics have borne fruit. Nikita obviously can't be sure Leggup will talk if tortured, or that once torture starts, making a deal will still be possible.

WHO HOLDS THE GOODS?

But Comcleansky isn't naive, so naturally he's concerned about being fed some false dope by Leggup. And if that happens, he doesn't want to have given up control of his prisoner before taking a crack at the torture route. So Comcleansky takes the position that he will turn Leggup over to Paavo Mekko, but only *after* it has been proved that the information Leggup provides is true.

That's bad news for Arthur, since what he's planning to reveal obviously won't pass muster. He has to squelch this concept fast.

"No, no," says Leggup. "The information I'm going to give you is correct. *[Unfortunately, Leggup has long since passed the point at which he can pretend that no information exists.]* But if I'm not in Finnish custody, it would be too easy for you guys to back out of the deal — and the Finns would lack both incentive and the means to pry me loose."

The reference to the Reds welshing prompts a sharp kick from Nikita's left boot, bruising Leggup's skin. Arthur winces, but continues:

"Here's what I suggest instead. Turn me over to the Finns at the time I give you the plan. In about a week, you'll know that it's correct. And you'll have an agreement with Mekko that if the information proves to be incorrect, the Finns will deliver me back to the KGB."

Leggup's proposal leads to considerable discussion back and forth. One particularly thorny issue is how to determine whether the information is correct. Leggup takes a firm position that this can't be based solely on the Soviets' say-so and suggests some impartial arbiter — a kind of international CPA. Comcleansky jabs at Leggup's groin with his swagger stick.

CONCOCTING A LOOPHOLE

Meanwhile, Leggup has another concern. Assume, *mirabile dictu,* that he's successful in persuading Nikita to turn him over to the Finns. Since Leggup *knows* his information will prove flawed, the mayor of Selhinki — who by now has arrived at KGB headquarters — might then feel duty-bound to return Leggup to the KGB. Arthur needs to work out a loophole in advance. So he asks for permission to speak to Mekko alone, citing as his reason the need to ascertain whether he can trust the Finnish official.

Comcleansky is suspicious but confident that Paavo Mekko won't do anything crooked. He allows Leggup and Mekko to stand alone in an open field, away from any bugging devices. *[For the movie version, I envision first a long shot across the frozen steppe — à la David Lean's "Dr. Zhivago" — zooming slowly into a tight close-up of the two figures conversing, their breath clearly visible in the frigid air. . . .]*

Leggup realizes it would be a mistake to let Mekko know that the information he proposes to give the KGB is false — Mekko might righteously refuse to be involved in a deal in which the Reds are being duped. So Leggup takes the following tack:

"Look here, Mayor, I'm worried that the KGB will *claim* that my information is false, just to get me back as a prisoner. I want to have an understanding with you that if the Soviets make that claim, I'll be permitted to present my case to a Finnish court and let the judge decide whether or not I've lied."

"This is fine with me," says Mekko, delighted to be taken off the hook.

Although no agreement has been reached on when Finnish custody is to begin, Leggup has already started thinking about the wording of the document. He will volunteer to draft the language — knowing the clear advantage that being the draftsman provides. His provisions will require the Finns to return him to KGB custody if he has given the Soviets "false information." In fact, Leggup intends to give the KGB information that is *true,* but irrelevant — having nothing to do with the Stolichnaya plot. With the ambiguity of the contractual language, plus his deal with Mekko to refer matters to a Finnish court, Leggup figures he can drag things out for at least a year — by which time, he's hopeful, the war will have ended.

BREAKING THE IMPASSE

But now, matters have slowed to a crawl. The parties are at an impasse. Comcleansky, suspicious about the information he will get, remains reluctant to turn Leggup over to Mekko until the information is proven correct. Leggup, knowing his information won't please the KGB, can't afford to remain in Soviet custody until the moment of truth. But how can he persuade the Reds to release him pending the determination? He needs a creative rationale.

"Aha!" Arthur's face lights up, as he ponders his new tactic. He requests a meeting with just Nikita; Paavo Mekko is excluded.

"Here's my problem," says Leggup to Comcleansky when they're alone. "I'm concerned about you guys, sure; but I'm just as worried about the *American* authorities. Hell, this is treason! Think what they'll do to me if they discover I've squealed to you."

Leggup now has Comcleansky's attention; Nikita hadn't previously considered this aspect.

"Let's say we do it *your* way," Leggup continues, "and wait until the information proves to be correct — which it will — before you release me. Then, when Mekko and I arrive in Selhinki right after the event, and Mekko writes his report to the Finnish authorities about what has happened — well, sure as I'm sitting here, the American ambassador will figure out what went on."

Captain is right about that, thinks Comcleansky.

"From the standpoint of the Americans not catching on," Arthur goes on, "It's much better to let me go with the mayor of Selhinki *now*. Since he won't have to return me to you (because the information will be true), his report won't have to deal with that contingency — and I won't have to face a U. S. firing squad."

Comcleansky is silent, assessing the possibilities.

"In fact, Nikita — I hope you don't mind me getting personal — I feel so strongly about this point that I'm going to make it a condition of our deal. As far as I'm concerned, it's a real deal-breaker."

An interesting point, thinks Comcleansky, as he idly runs his gloved hand along the length of the rack, simulating the creaking sounds of a stretched human body. *Still, am not yet convinced. . . .*

*   *   *

So — what do you think? Does Nikita relent? Can Leggup make it into Finland? Will the Stolichnaya distillery be destroyed?

Buy the novel.

INDEX

B

E

F

H